A Groundling's Guide

to Shakespeare's *Hamlet*

Hilary Kovar Justice

Story Spring Publishing, LLC
Cincinnati, Ohio

Story Spring Publishing, LLC
P.O. Box 9727
Cincinnati, OH 45209
www.storyspringpublishing.com

Book Layout adapted from ©2013 BookDesignTemplates.com.
Cover and Interior Illustration: "Folio Hamlet" ©2014 Elizabeth E. Schuch, Immortal Longings, London.

Ordering Information:
Quantity sales. Special discounts are available on quantity purchases by schools, associations, and others. For details, contact the "Special Sales Department" at the address above.

A Groundling's Guide to Shakespeare's *Hamlet*/Hilary Kovar Justice. —1st ed.
ISBN 978-1-940699-06-6

This work is dedicated
with affection and gratitude
to my first Shakespeare teacher

Tim Averill

Contents

Acknowledgments

This guide is the result of uncountable moments in classrooms in which I have been both student and teacher, in rehearsal spaces in which I have been both actor and director, and conversations occurring everywhere, for everyone seems to have opinions on and ideas about Shakespeare generally and *Hamlet* in particular.

This guide owes its existence to two people: Tim Averill, my English teacher at Manchester High School from 1979-1984, whose patience, contagious enthusiasm, and pride as I moved from extreme Shakespeare fear to utter excitement at the possibilities of Shakespeare's language (which shift occurred as we read *Hamlet*) inspires my teaching to this day; and Professor David Bevington, whose teaching assistant and dissertation student I had the privilege of being, and whose graciousness and finely honed mind inspire my reading, research, and writing as a Humanities scholar and mentor.

As a Master's student, I was herded into David's presence by Professors Milla Riggio and Arthur Feinsod of Trinity College (Hartford) during rehearsals for *The Winter's Tale*, in which I played Hermione. Clad in a dirty, bloody toga (in which my character had just given birth and collapsed on a none-too-clean stage at the news that her son was dead), I made my way into the audience, saying, "I've been told I'm supposed to talk to you about Ph.D. programs. I'm supposedly dead right now, but I don't want to take you away from Act IV." "I don't really like Act IV anyway," he said, encouraging me to apply to the University of Chicago for my Ph.D. At that point, my fear was the GREs. "Have you seen the Shakespeare questions? They're impossible!" "Oh, dear—I *am* sorry," he replied, then he smiled. "I wrote them."

I was accepted anyway.

I have since taught and continued to study *Hamlet* with high school and university students, all of whom have met the challenge of becoming better readers of Shakespeare and informed my understanding of the play. I owe each of them much, especially my students at Illinois State University, but they are far too numerous to mention here, so I will mention only a recent three whose readings have most influenced my own: Yu Jia (whose translations lent layers of nuance to my understanding of Shakespeare's language); Genevieve Krabbe (whose understanding of Ophelia completely changed my reading of III.i); and A.J. Harris (whose fascination with Marcellus and his function in the play resulted in the title of this guide). Three decades after I wrestled with Shakespeare Fear in Tim Averill's Shakespeare class, these three students enrolled in my Drama class. I thank them and all of my students for proving that, as Jane Austen once said of the English village, there is always something new to be learned in studying Shakespeare.

I also wish to thank my colleagues at Illinois State University for their recognition that a scholar of American Literature and Textual Studies once had a previous life as a Shakespearean actor and director, providing me the opportunity to pursue that absolutely urgent curiosity and passion: Christopher Breu, Katherine Ellison, Cynthia Huff, Tim Hunt, Tara Lyons, Bob McLaughlin, Rhonda Nicol, Torri Thompson, and especially Ricardo Cortez Cruz, who ensured that this guide, developed for a teaching pinch-hit, saw a second round.

I am grateful to Richard (Ric) Gilbert, David Bareford, and Victor Bayona of R&D Choreography (Chicago) for working with generations of Illinois State University English majors to bring the end of the play to life during our semester-end workshops. A good swordfight is a great way to end an intense semester, and I look forward to many more such collaborations. Special thanks to Libby Lind for her miracle-working in finding us performance space in a building better suited to round-table discussion and writing in computer labs. If our swashbuckling has damaged any ceiling tiles, it is not her doing.

To all of my friends and colleagues in my former life as a theater person, a fond smile and a standing ovation. John Stuart, Ellen Noonan, David Brown, Tom McDonough, Ann Suchoza McDonough, Carol Cullen Smith, Tina Chalmers, Jamie Potry, Jesse Robbins, Joe Pangratz, Celeste Therrien Ryfa, and especially Anne Brennan contributed much to my understanding of theater and its creation of transitory communities whose impressions last a lifetime.

A particular mention of utmost importance is due Rebecca Kovar, who, the night before I taught *Hamlet* for the first time at the university level, spontaneously burst into a mock lecture beginning, "So there's this guy, see…" The tag-line "But we'll get to that later" is still a refrain in our friendship; I look forward to many more years of that "later."

My deepest thanks to Diane Tarbuck, Barbara Tarbuck, and Jennifer Correa at Story Spring Publishing for their painstaking precision and for their support when topic saturation warred with scope creep. If one problem with Shakespeare is knowing where to start, another is deciding when to stop.

A tip of the hat to my students Elise Robertson and Elora Karim for their enthusiasm, courage, and eagle-eyed attention to detail, and a grace note to Katie Koehler for proving how very beautifully a novice reader of Shakespeare can grow in a single, short semester.

As always, a final nod of gratitude to my friends and family, who by now are used to my disappearing down the rabbit hole of scholarship and writing and stand by to toss encouragement, snark, Bela Karolyi quotes, and occasionally food into my vicinity from a safe distance. In addition to Rebecca, Rhonda, and Ann, already mentioned above, my thanks to Stacia McClure-Blome, Mary Lou Freitag, Jessica Aldis, Susan Beegel, Anicee Dowling, and especially and always Michele Budden, whose fluency with the whats, the hows, and the whys is preternatural and divinely inspired. A tip of the hat to my writing group, Write Side Up: PJ, Lin, Scoffy, Libby, Wendy, Mara, Juni, Dicky, Annie, and Tricie.

Not even Shakespeare could capture in words (and thus would leave silent space for) the profound joy, wonder, and blessing that is my family—my mother, Norma Seim, and my husband, David Kovar. Here is that silence:

Part 1

How to Read
Shakespeare

Introduction

On Becoming a Groundling: The How of Shakespeare

WHY ANOTHER GUIDE to Shakespeare?

Guides to Shakespeare's plays are most often shortcuts straight to the what—what is being said, who says what to whom, what happens, etc. But no shortcut series exists that talks about how—and with Shakespeare, the how reveals the what. Understanding how his characters speak reveals more about what they're saying (and why, and who they are) than any short-cut study guide, and without losing nuance, or wonder, or joy.

This study guide is intended for the serious reader of Shakespeare— the reader who wants to engage with the language, to overcome "Shakespeare fear," to watch the text bloom from the page, abounding with endless possibilities, readings, and decisions that the reader (or actor, or director, or audience member) must make as part of engaging with the production of the play.

Shakespeare's plays were intended to be produced—to be fully realized on the stage, where they would be seen and most importantly heard by his original audience, comprised of a microcosm of Elizabethan society. Most students of Shakespeare have at least heard of the groundlings, those in the lowest orders of society who stood on the floor at the Globe to witness the play at eye level. The groundlings were by and large uneducated and often illiterate, but neither is synonymous with stupid: the continued survival of the Globe depended largely on the groundlings' patronage, and no theater ever stayed open by insulting its audience.

Shakespeare's respect for the groundlings—and for commonsense wisdom—is but one feature that comes clear when reading his plays like an actor preparing for a role.

But his plays are over four centuries old, and language, media consumption, common knowledge, and cultural referents have undergone radical transformation and almost unchartable evolution since the days of the Globe and the groundlings, and present-day readers have to work to achieve the level of understanding the groundlings could claim by birthright.

We can equal the groundlings with practice, and therein lies this guide.

The groundlings lived within a primarily aural culture; there is as much to be found in the sound of Shakespeare's language as in footnotes that explain vocabulary, literary and historical references, and archaisms that but for scholars would be otherwise lost. These footnotes are crucial for any reader of Shakespeare (with the possible exception of the experts, whose intricate contestations are but one of the many joys inspired by his works), but although the information they provide is necessary, it comprises only one amongst many innate fluencies his Elizabethan audience possessed.

Aural fluency is one; another is the fluency inhering in the difference between reading words on a page and attending—or participating in—performance on stage.

Shakespeare spoken aloud requires thousands of decisions per play. When does one pause; when does one interrupt; when does one engage in rapid-fire dialogue exchange—and, in all cases, why? How does one know?

The groundlings would not have needed to decide; performers make those decisions and portray them.

So, how is a performer to know?

The answer lies in page layout—which requires that present-day readers of Shakespeare know how to read the blank margin spaces as well as the text.

This guide provides instruction there as well.

Knowing where to look and listen, where to spot silence and tone, knowing how to read Shakespeare—all these inspire confidence, which mitigate the "Shakespeare fear" that prevents educators, students, and readers alike from really enjoying the great fun to be found in the plays. There are things you can know for sure about Shakespeare after learning only a very few terms and after only a little bit of practice.

What you can know for sure provides a foundation for the far more interesting things you can't know, because the text doesn't provide those answers. The printed text, that is; a performance, a different "text," must provide answers to those questions, lest the play seem to deflate and collapse in on itself (as many productions do, especially of *Hamlet*). Read fluently, Shakespearean plays are rife with ambiguity; questions lead to more questions, which lead to yet more. The identification of some of these questions is possible only when you know what you can know for sure. The rest follow fluidly as individual hearts and minds pursue them toward concrete resolution or deliberate ambiguity.

The choices actors and directors make as they engage these questions collectively determine what a given production of *Hamlet* will convey to its audience. What stance will a production take on insanity? On suicide? On power, honor, and relationships? On gender? What follows is a brief introduction to some of the high-stakes ambiguities and questions that confront actors playing

Gertrude, Ophelia, and Hamlet. Each question leads to more questions, which will be explored throughout this guide.

How much does Gertrude know?

A central ambiguity in *Hamlet* is Gertrude. Does she know about Claudius's crimes? Was she complicit? Does she remain clueless, an empty vacuity of vague maternal worry, with no spine, ending as another ignorant victim of Claudius's machinations? Or does she at some point start to suspect Claudius, suspect that there is more method than madness in her son, begin to realize her own culpability in that madness? When she drinks from the poisoned cup at the end, does she know it contains poison? Suspect? Is it suicide committed in vapid ignorance, or a noble sacrifice made by a mother to protect her son (however in vain)? The text doesn't say. When Claudius tells her not to drink, the text provides only this:

> "I will, my lord. I pray you, pardon me" (V.ii.294).*

To whom is this line addressed? Claudius? God? Is the first part addressed to one character—perhaps Claudius—and the second to another—perhaps Hamlet? The possibilities are endless. The text doesn't say, but the actors and director must know.

Note on Shakespearean citation: The formal citation for Act V, scene ii, line 294 is rendered: V.ii.294.

How much does Ophelia know?

A similar ambiguity lies in Ophelia's character. Is she the good, virginal daughter throughout, obedient and unquestioning? Or does she, like the more dynamic version of Gertrude explored above, begin to suspect the larger machinations of her own father and then, perhaps, of the King? When she returns Hamlet's tokens at her father's command, she knows that Polonius and Claudius are secreted nearby, spying. When Hamlet asks her, "Where's your father?" (III.i.131), she must respond, "At home, my lord" (III.i.132), but does she reveal her lie with her eyes? Accidentally? Deliberately? Hamlet and Ophelia both know they are being spied on; they must play their roles as required by duty (Ophelia to her father and King; Hamlet to his own larger purpose), but the scene becomes much more interesting if they both knowingly sacrifice their love for the good of Denmark. How much more profound her lament, "Oh, what a noble mind is here o'erthrown!" (III.i.153) if she blames not Hamlet's supposed madness (as most productions would have it) but the King and, by extension, her own father.

But the script doesn't say.

The fact that it doesn't is interesting. Very interesting. Whereas it is tempting to impose 21st-century assumptions regarding the benighted block-headedness with which the laws of Elizabethan England dealt with gender issues onto Shakespeare's personal beliefs, his plays suggest otherwise. It would have been unwise for him to critique social norms too aggressively—my earlier point about the economic survival of the Globe stands here—but questions regarding his female characters that go unanswered by the text seem the very questions worth exploring.

To what extent could Shakespeare publicly gesture toward cultural critique without getting shut down? His oeuvre suggests he could and did do so liberally, if often obliquely.

The fact that Ophelia's gown—the sartorial indicator of her gender and her status as marriage-aged woman, not girl—is what finally drowns her is richly suggestive on that point.

Was Shakespeare saying that to be a woman is to be doomed by one's own skirts?

Isn't that powerlessness what Lady Macbeth laments when she says, "unsex me here" *Macbeth* (I.v.41)?

Other assumptions present-day readers bring to *Hamlet* are also worth noting, some of which have answers lurking in the text, some of which do not.

The highest-stakes question for readers of *Hamlet* involve Hamlet himself.

Hamlet: To kill or not to kill?

Is Hamlet crazy?

Possibly—but perhaps not as crazy as one might think. The evidence is in the page margins. (This will be explained more fully in this guide, in the section on poetry versus prose.)

Is Hamlet suicidal?

Again, possibly—but perhaps not as actively or as deeply suicidal as a superficial reading might suggest. Evidence? When is a soliloquy not a soliloquy? (This will be explained more fully as well, in the section on III.i.)

Another question, thanks to Mel Gibson's 1990 movie version in which Hamlet and Gertrude share an utterly unscripted kiss: Does Hamlet have an Oedipal attraction to his own mother?

No. The play references incest, but it is incest-in-law: Claudius, like Henry VIII before him, should not have married his dead brother's widow. To do so was to marry his sister-*in-law*; the incest there is legally defined, not biologically.

Perhaps the most erroneous assumption of all in current play amongst first-time readers and audience members is this: the assumption that Hamlet is supposed to be the King—his father's dead; he's the prince; primogeniture demands that he be King! And he sits by and doesn't kick Claudius off the throne despite (obviously) despising him.

Hamlet does nothing. What a weak character. What a procrastinator. He can't do *anything*.

Except, no. The succession laws in Denmark, as evidenced by Claudius's monologue in the opening of Act I, scene ii, were not based on primogeniture. The eldest son need not inherit; succession in Denmark operates according to tanistry—the same method whereby clan chiefs are chosen in Scotland: The current clan chief selects his heir from amongst his male relatives and announces his choice before his "court." And Scotland and succession were much on the minds of *Hamlet*'s initial audience; the heir to the by-then definitely childless Queen Elizabeth I was James VI of Scotland, son of Mary, Queen of Scots.

If Hamlet is weak and a do-nothing procrastinator, it's not because Claudius is on a throne that should be Hamlet's.

Yet the fact remains that Hamlet—to his own increasing frustration—takes no confrontational action against Claudius for the first half of the play. No question. He doesn't.

Why? The fast answer is that he doesn't want to risk his own immortal soul, but there is a longer, more illuminating exploration cued by two minute textual details: One involves the names "Rosencrantz" and "Guildenstern." The other is Wittenberg.

This is the sort of wondering this guide invites readers to notice and consider (and enhances skills for doing both):

First, the names:

Unlike the names Cornelius and Voltimand (the play's other "throw-away" pair of characters), the names Rosencrantz and Guildenstern read as Jewish. (Cornelius reads Latinate; Voltimand, Germanic.) Why do we suddenly have two Jewish characters in the middle of the court of Denmark? Elizabethan anti-Semitism is evident in Claudius's inability to tell the two characters apart (for so their introduction scene [II.ii] is often played, with Gertrude correcting his error); even so, their names seem out of pattern on the *dramatis personae* list.

The pattern break—two Jewish-sounding names introduced relatively late in the midst of the play's established Latinate (Cornelius, Claudius, Polonius), Italianate (Ophelia, Horatio), and Germanic (Gertrude, Voltimand) "norm"—and the aural catchiness exploited by Tom Stoppard in *Rosencrantz and Guildenstern are Dead*—beg further exploration.

Rosencrantz—the name:

Starting with "Rosencrantz": The first syllable, "rose," has an obvious current English meaning; "crantz" functions as a homonym for a now archaic word that the play provides in original context at V.i.232: "crants," the crown of flowers that adorned the grave of a virgin (Ophelia). To Shakespeare's original auditors, then, the name would aurally suggest "rose crown," "crown of roses," "crown of thorns." Interesting.

Guildenstern—the name:

The first syllable, "guild," likewise has a current English meaning— the guild structure of tradesmen's crafts of medieval Europe (*e.g.*, the goldsmiths' guild, the tanners' guild, etc.). The last syllable, "stern," ditto—"stern," meaning dour or hard. Craft/trade/work, stern/dour/hard combine to suggest "hard work," "stern work ethic," etc.

Two Jewish-sounding names, which socio-ethnically invokes the concept of theology, one with easily audible reference to Christ's crown of thorns, the other with reference to hard work, encompass the crisis of the Protestant Revolution (or Reformation) of the previous century, in which the path to God was contested—Is the path to the Christian Heaven via faith or works? Interesting. Very interesting.

Wittenberg—the university:

This is made even more interesting by considering Hamlet's university—Wittenberg—which was a major if not the center of continental Protestant thought; Martin Luther was on the faculty in the early 16ᵗʰ century (about 100 years before *Hamlet* was first performed). In common, popular knowledge (of the sort the groundlings might possess), Martin Luther provided the catalyst for that religious schism by nailing his "Ninety-Five Theses" to the door of All Saints' Church in Wittenberg.

Propositional Logic and "Philosophy":

The rhetorical structure of Luther's "Theses" is that of propositional logic: Given/If-Then/Therefore. This method of "proof" is now commonly taught as part of a mathematics curriculum. Not long ago, however, propositional logic belonged more centrally to departments of philosophy (where it can sometimes still be found). When Hamlet tells Horatio in I.v, "There are more things in heaven and earth... than are dreamt of in your philosophy" (I.v.175-76), he doesn't necessarily mean Horatio's personal philosophy, but rather philosophy as studied at Wittenberg: deploying propositional logic in the service of resolving the theological "faith versus works" debate. When confronted with central theological questions such as "Can humans know God?" "If so, are they obligated to try?" and "If so, what is the best method to use?" Wittenberg's answer to the latter was "propositional logic."

Propositional logic is the deductive method which, once spotted, so overtly governs the first three acts of *Hamlet* in the service of protecting Hamlet's immortal soul that all questions of "procrastination" and "whining" are rendered as anachronistic as Freud's Oedipal theory to what Shakespeare wrote. Hamlet faces a very personal version of the question that divided Europe for much of the sixteenth century: Should he believe the Ghost unquestioningly (a question of faith and emotion) or should he trust his soul only to evidence (a question of works; by reason and proof shall Hamlet finally know Claudius's actions)?

The Given/If-Then/Therefore structure of propositional logic governs the play's main plot and various subplots, eventually emerging as the basis for many of the characters' thought processes, schemes, and approaches to understanding their world.

The largest instance is the challenge Hamlet faces in determining his course of action:

GIVEN that there is a Ghost walking around in his father's shape,

IF the Ghost is truly the ghost of Hamlet's father,

THEN Claudius is a murderer,

THEREFORE Hamlet must kill Claudius to avenge his father's death.

But:

IF the Ghost is not the ghost of Hamlet's father,

THEN the Ghost is a demon sent from Hell to tempt Hamlet into a mortal sin,

THEREFORE Hamlet must not kill Claudius.

The problem is an absolute binary. To kill or not to kill? That is actually the question Hamlet must answer; his efforts to answer it comprise the first half of the play.

Like a good scholar, he deploys the best of his training in the service of a question that will affect not only his country but his immortal soul (with which he is much preoccupied, which makes sense). He sets up a series of logical equations which bring him ever closer to the proof he needs to resolve the mutually exclusive binary identity of the Ghost. IF I act crazy, and IF Claudius is guilty, THEN Claudius may become unsettled enough to reveal his guilt. Claudius sends for Rosencrantz and Guildenstern—indication that the King is unsettled, but not evidence of innocence or guilt. Meanwhile, IF I act crazy to Ophelia, and IF she reports it to her father, THEN Claudius will believe I am crazy (evidence of the truth of Hamlet's affection for Ophelia), and THEN the King may become unsettled enough to reveal his guilt.

When Ophelia lies to Hamlet in III.i with her line, "At home, my lord" (whether or not she reveals the truth with her eyes or expression), Hamlet knows the paths by which information travels in Denmark, knows he is being spied on, etc. Meanwhile, his "seeming" crazy provides an inky cloak of concealment for his larger purpose: eliciting the truth about Claudius. Hamlet's final piece of evidence is planted with another "If-then" statement: "*If* 'a do blench,/ I know my course" (emphasis added; II.ii.598-99).

The truth is revealed in III.ii, when Claudius stands and stops the play, *The Murder of Gonzago*; this resolves the initial propositional logic question set forth in Act I:

GIVEN that Claudius is guilty,

THEREFORE the Ghost is Hamlet's father and not a demon of temptation, and

THEREFORE Hamlet must kill Claudius.

At least through III.ii, Hamlet's delay hasn't been a delay at all; he has been resolving a high-stakes question using propositional logic in the service of detective work. Not procrastination, not whining, not at all a do-nothing prince, but rather a cerebral one, putting forth the best of his intellect and training in the service of his country, his father, and his immortal soul.

Once you've spotted it, propositional logic is everywhere in the play—in Polonius's plot to ensnare Hamlet (and more power for himself) via love for his daughter (Polonius's logic is perfect; his assumptions are flawed); in Claudius's presentation of his plans for the final duel as he describes them to Laertes (Claudius's logic is likewise flawless; the truth of his assumptions is murky—does Hamlet agree to the duel based on jealousy, as Claudius opines he must, or does

Hamlet agree to the duel out of an innate sense of honor and justice, owing Laertes his own likely humiliation in a mock trial by combat because he really did kill Laertes's father).

"Rosencrantz," "Guildenstern," "Wittenberg," and philosophy— four words that in their original performance would not have required a Humanities scholar to unpack their aural and cultural resonances. Their aural resonances and cultural referents would have been instantly available to a groundling with working ears and the most distant nodding acquaintance with recent European history, a history whose central question contributed directly to putting Queen Elizabeth I on the English throne.

One of the purposes of this guide, then, is to invite readers to think like a groundling. When any line—almost any word—can bloom under creative, informed scrutiny, where to start? The options are so numerous as to be daunting, indeed, but a beauty of creative endeavor is that it allows for experimentation and play. A decision regarding Gertrude in Act I may help resolve an ambiguity for Ophelia in Act III; both impact Hamlet and will affect choices regarding his character in Act V. This guide invites readers to imagine how a production results from the accumulation of countless individual decisions and how different decisions yield vastly different, equally powerful productions under the umbrella of the single title, *Hamlet.*

Another purpose of this guide is to introduce readers to the intricacies of Shakespeare's language practices. Not vocabulary, which can be found in footnotes and glossaries both in print and online, but practices, with emphasis on the aural and the performative. By introducing a very few concepts from poetry, rhetoric, and print-formatting, as well as a very few dramatic terms, this guide offers readers a useful key to mapping their own informed reading of text. Study guide questions keyed to each scene identify likely places to pause, explore, and practice—curiosity calisthenics for people determined to become better readers of Shakespeare.

Shakespeare fear is real, and fear leads to shortcuts, to squelching curiosity, to stifling the pleasures, laughter, and wonder that require only a bit of practice to begin to enjoy. Shakespeare fear exists because people don't believe they can read Shakespeare, and too much current teaching of Shakespeare perpetuates rather than erases this fear, because teachers feel it, too. No one can read Shakespeare perfectly the first time; there is no shame in being a beginner or in starting over, in noticing new things, in wondering how and where to start.

This guide provides that how—at least one version of it.

Figuring out what Shakespearean characters are saying is necessary. The best way to start is to figure out how they're saying it. This may seem counterintuitive, but it works. "How" leads more directly to "what" (and "why") than any set of footnotes can or should attempt to. That's vocabulary; that's reference. Both are crucial, but no one ever learned a language by memorizing individual words or sayings.

Shakespeare's writing challenges readers to engage with dynamic relationships in a fluid system of word, sound, character, concept, and culture. Perfect fluency may not be possible; none of us are native Elizabethans. But with effort, readers can approach the aural fluency of a groundling—we can learn to hear the text and thus to imagine it in performance, to be a participatory auditor, to collaborate actively in the thousand and one decisions that go into a fully realized reading of a play. There is no fourth wall in Shakespeare; there is nothing to keep the groundlings out. It is theater for and with the groundlings, who, innately fluent with the "how" of Shakespeare, could easily enjoy the "what" of each particular play.

This is a guide—not *the* guide; *a* guide—to the how as it is practiced by actors preparing and exploring Shakespeare for performance; the "whats" change with each play, but the "hows" are the same for all of them. Engaged collaboration with the particulars of the text allows a reader to approximate a performance—which is how the groundlings experienced Shakespeare's plays; experience with one text makes the next one easier. Practice makes the play.

Actors, language, and a stage; groundlings with ears, eyes, and hearts. Their collective how is what made Shakespeare Shakespeare.

How to Use This Guide

Before beginning the play:

Acquire the matching edition.

This guide is specifically keyed to the language, line numbers, and footnotes in *Four Tragedies: Hamlet, Othello, King Lear, Macbeth*, edited by David Bevington and David Scott Kastan (updated 2005), which is inexpensive and widely available. Readers of other editions may experience confusion and frustration with some of the study questions, as line numbers and footnotes will not match, and things will fall apart quickly from there. As the purpose of this guide is to render Shakespeare more comprehensible and more enjoyable, and using a different edition is likely to make things more difficult and less pleasurable, using the matching edition is key.

Read the "Introduction: On Becoming a Groundling" (page 1).

This guide offers many things, but not everything. The introduction outlines what it does and doesn't do—and how, and why. The introduction also contains substantive information to which subsequent sections of this guide refer, although to accommodate readers' various points of entry, some of that information is repeated elsewhere.

Refer as needed to the "How to Read Shakespeare" section (page 23).

This section introduces important concepts and terms in three categories (Drama, Language, and Aurality), defining them according to how they contribute to understanding Shakespeare. Baseline norms are identified; discussions of variations and exceptions follow. The sections devoted to each act (and the study guide questions contained therein) are designed to build fluency with using these terms to identify likely fruitful moments for consideration and exploration.

It is recommended but not necessary to read the sections on Drama, Language, and Aurality before beginning the play, but they do provide extended discussion of terms used throughout this guide.

Working through the play:

Reading the play (suggestions):

Read each scene through, aloud, if possible, referring as needed to the footnotes in the text.

Next, read the study guide questions for the scene, referring to other sections (especially the Glossary) as needed.

Then read the scene again.

Only then begin to work through the study guide questions.

Developing aural fluency (suggestions):

Listen to a professional production of the play. Audio-only is best (YouTube with the screen darkened is convenient) lest acting decisions, casting, costuming, set design, and other production elements foreclose possibility. Each production must resolve many of the play's ambiguities, and as the resolutions are often not found in the text, they are presented visually.

"To be or not to be": There are several versions of Hamlet's "To be or not to be" speech (III.i.57-91) available on YouTube; it's an excellent moment in the play to pause and consider the tremendous variations supported by a single text. Classic versions to search for include Lawrence Olivier (1948) and Richard Burton (1964); more recent versions worth comparing include performances by Mel Gibson (1990), Kenneth Branagh (1996), and David Tennant (2009). The use of this speech in *The King's Speech* (2010), in which it is performed by Colin Firth, offers a particularly rich statement on language and leadership; countless other references to this speech exist, and all are worth exploring and considering.

Refer as needed to the "Characters" section (page 51).

The Characters section includes brief notes on all named characters and their relationships to the play's central questions and recurring issues. Ambiguities with which readers, actors, and directors must engage are introduced here as a series of questions.

It is not necessary to read this section before beginning to work through the play; it is organized alphabetically to facilitate quick reference as needed.

Work through the study guides and questions for each act.

The sections devoted to each act begin with a general introduction designed to ground the reader in the play's unfolding story, plot, and structure. These introductory moments highlight elements that will receive more detailed attention and exploration in the study guide questions that follow. Sections devoted to Acts I and III are presented in two parts, each covering half of the act, in order to encourage especially detailed attention—to Act I because it introduces the play; to Act III because of its specific structural features on which the play's resolution depends. Act III is the mountain to scale; after Act III, many possibilities are foreclosed, and nearly everyone's path to the end is clear.

These sections present study questions to consider and explore. Questions are presented chronologically and are designed to be read as side-by-side companions to the text of the play. These questions are for the most part open-ended and offered for exploration (although some do have technical right/wrong aspects which are introduced in the "How to Read Shakespeare" section). Questions ask readers to focus their attention on and to explore brief passages, lines, language features, structural features, and dramatic moments. Collectively, the study questions function as an opportunity to consider each scene as an accretion of minute details and decisions which, taken together, comprise an informed, nuanced reading of the play. The study questions sequentially introduce and develop various skills that, with practice, promote fluency with Shakespeare's language.

The number and open-endedness of these questions comprise a daunting but do-able challenge to the dedicated student; advanced undergraduate English majors have successfully completed this guide on the following schedule:

Week 1: Drama, Language, and Aurality (presented in class with examples to explore)

Week 2: Act I (50 questions, evenly distributed)

Week 3: Act II (all questions)

Week 4: Act III.i-ii (all questions)

Week 5: Act III.iii-iv (all questions)

Week 6: Act IV (50 questions, evenly distributed)

Week 7: Act V (all questions)

Week 8: Culminative Project:
"The Royal Medical Examiner" or "Character Diaries"

Week 9: Page-to-Stage Workshop, V.ii

My students call this experience "Shakespeare with the gloves off." It is difficult, intense, and a tremendous challenge to students and instructor alike, but by Week 4 (which begins Act III), new and returning readers of Shakespeare almost always experience a sea change in sensitivity to nuance, openness to contradictory textually-supported readings, commitment, confidence, pleasure, and passion. Students who are often initially skeptical ("We're spending over two months on one play?") by Act III frequently wish for more time to do more, to read more closely, to discuss more thoroughly, to explore more deeply and with greater range.

Almost any one of the study guide questions can fuel an entire period of class discussion, can provide the kernel of a full-length character analysis, or can serve as an embarkation for a final essay, scholarly article, or life-long curiosity.

> *A note to classroom instructors: Completing all of the included study guide questions requires an ideal freedom of time. Selecting an even distribution of questions from the sections devoted to each act will ensure complete coverage; study guide questions follow the unfolding of each scene chronologically.*

Refer as needed to the Glossary.

The Glossary presents the terms from the "How to Read Shakespeare" section, alphabetized and with abbreviated definitions, for ease of reference.

Complete a culminating project.

Two possible options for a culminating project are outlined which are designed to offer creativity free rein in occasions of serious, well-informed fun. The first option involves adopting the role of Royal Medical Examiner to the Court of His Majesty, Fortinbras I. The second proposes several approaches to the creation of characters' private diaries and personal papers, including not only named characters but those of the unnamed castle servants, soldiers, and members of the court with which any royal castle must be populated, even if we barely (if ever) glimpse them on stage.

How to Read Shakespeare: Drama, Language, and Aurality

ALTHOUGH EDITORS OF Shakespeare provide excellent footnotes, these are most often concerned with vocabulary, archaisms, and historical or literary references with which contemporary readers cannot be expected to be familiar. These footnotes are invaluable for comprehension, yet (for reasons of page space and volume size) editors can rarely devote ample space to more than a brief introduction of how to do more with Shakespeare's language: how to analyze poetic meter (a process called "scansion") and other aural poetic features; how to spot and evaluate various rhetorical and dramatic devices; how to understand various page layout practices; and how to begin to incorporate the information that all of these can provide to readers, actors, directors, and teachers of Shakespeare's work. These features are invitations to pause and explore more deeply, right here, right now, these words, these phrases, even these blank spaces. These features are the "X" that marks the spot of where to start "digging," or playing with the play. (It is called a "play" for a reason.)

This section, therefore, provides a brief introduction to the various additional kinds of information present on the page. Such an introduction is usually given to actors portraying Shakespearean characters, for whom making sense of and discovering nuance in the printed word comprises much of their primary responsibility. Developing such intimate familiarity with Shakespeare's language takes time and a bit of practice, but practice builds confidence (always desirable), and the "light bulb" moment when an "out there" reading of a phrase or a passage proves not only plausible but resonates throughout the entire play—when the text "blooms"—is its own limitless reward.

It is a rare luxury to have and take the time to consider any Shakespeare play as thoroughly and as closely as actors preparing for performance, but practice with that kind of work provides tremendous opportunity for learning, freedom, and joy. This section introduces and explains many of the features on which actors spend much of their preparation time, organized by kind (metric features, aural features, rhetorical features, etc.). The study guide questions that follow point readers to instances of these features as they occur throughout the text of the play, highlighting moments to pause and explore the limitless possibilities offered in a seemingly static text.

For ease of use, these features are also listed alphabetically in the Glossary that follows the study guide questions.

The key to identifying good places to pause and explore possibilities inherent in detail is remembering that Shakespeare's baseline forms are dialogue, blank verse, and iambic pentameter. These baseline forms and their variants are explained, with examples, in what follows.

Citing Shakespeare

Quotations from Shakespeare are cited by act, scene, and line number(s) as given in the following example: "How cheerfully on the false trail they cry!" (IV.v.112). Quotations covering multiple lines include a slash between lines: "How came he dear? I'll not be juggled with./ To hell, allegiance! Vows, to the blackest devil!" (IV.v.133-34).

Drama: Concepts, Terms, and Features

SHAKESPEAREAN TRAGEDY

Shakespeare's tragedy has quite a bit in common with its ancestor, Athenian tragedy—a hero facing a dilemma, the resolution of that dilemma resulting in some catharsis for hero and audience. The key word there is "dilemma." Current usage of "tragedy" is as a synonym for "very, very sad"; its use in drama is somewhat more specific. For a play to be a tragedy, the protagonist must face a dilemma (from the Greek "di-," meaning "two," and "lemma," meaning "horns"—thus "on the horns of a dilemma"), a "damned if you do; damned if you don't" situation. With the Ghost's Act I injunction to Hamlet to avenge his death but not judge Gertrude harshly (it's a bit late for that) or hurt her in any way, Hamlet faces a perfect dilemma: assuming he can ascertain Claudius's guilt and thus the Ghost's actual identity (father's spirit or demon of temptation), he cannot kill Claudius without hurting Gertrude. It's impossible.

Shakespearean tragedies—at least three of the major four (*Othello, Macbeth, Hamlet,* and *King Lear*)—share a distinct remarkable feature of returning to a recurring pair of very simple words and elaborating on the figurative and conceptual possibilities inherent in these distilled pairs. In *Macbeth,* the pair is "hand" and man"; the play asks what makes a man: what he does (hand) or what he is (man). In *King Lear,* the pair is "eye" and "heart"; the play asks which should man follow: the truth he can see (eye) or the truth he can feel (heart). If there is a pair in *Othello,* I've not yet found it—there may very well be.

Hamlet is occasionally referred to as Shakespeare's "most perfect tragedy" perhaps because the essential pair is "love" and "duty"—the perfect Classical dilemma—existing under a nearly synonymous and nearly transparent veil of an additional pair which together tore

Renaissance Europe apart: "faith" and "works." Love/duty and faith/works occur in proximity almost everywhere in *Hamlet*; it's great fun to try to spot them and tease out their nuanced inflections in various scenes, situations, and contexts.

SHAKESPEAREAN STRUCTURE

Shakespeare's plays involve a five-act structure. A scene changes when all of the characters exit and a new set of characters enters.

The Turn

In Western literature, the turn is the moment at which that which was previously only possible becomes either inevitable or impossible; usually occurs at or near the exact middle of a text (which, in Shakespeare, is often but not always III.ii, thus its alternative name, "the III.ii turn"). The turn in *Hamlet* occurs in III.ii. Prior to Claudius's silent admission of guilt, the question driving the play is "What will Hamlet do?" After that moment, Hamlet's course is obvious: he must try to kill Claudius. After the turn, the question that drives the play is "What will Claudius do?"

This structural feature extends far beyond the boundaries of Shakespeare; the turn in the *Harry Potter* series (the middle of which is the fourth book, *Harry Potter and the Goblet of Fire*) is the return of Voldemort to corporeal form, after which a final confrontation between him and Harry isn't just possible, it's inevitable.

FOILS & FOIL RELATIONSHIPS

When two characters, pairs of characters, or situations bear multiple strong similarities, they are said to be foils of each other or to exist in a foil relationship. Foil relationships allow a reader to isolate a difference—usually a single one—that conventionally accounts for and allows for deeper thinking on the effects of that single difference. For example, Hamlet, Sr., (the Ghost) and Claudius constitute an obvious foil relationship: They are brothers, both Kings of Denmark, both husbands of Gertrude, and they even look somewhat alike. However, one is Hamlet's father, and one is not, and thereon hangs an entire play.

Pairs of characters can also exist in foil relationships; Cornelius and Voltimand may be considered foils for Rosencrantz and Guildenstern—not individually, but collectively. Larger groups, especially families, countries, and situations, also offer foils. For example, the royal houses of Denmark and Norway are foils for each other; in both houses, the first kings are now deceased; both kings share names with their surviving sons; their brothers, both in some way "sick" or "diseased," now sit on the thrones. The salient difference is that whereas the royal house of Norway mentions no mother/wife/queen, the royal house of Denmark most emphatically does. This is Shakespeare's way of subtly underscoring Gertrude's centrality (at least emotional centrality) to the play.

BASELINE FORM: DIALOGUE

The baseline form of Shakespearean plays is dialogue, in which two or more characters converse. All departures from this baseline are worth pausing to consider more closely.

Variants (Single Speaker):

Monologue: A longish speech by a character when other characters are present. (For example, Claudius's speech to the court at I.ii.1-38 is a monologue.) Characters delivering monologues may be knowingly lying or spinning the truth, but not necessarily; the degree of truthfulness depends on character and context.

Soliloquy: A longish speech by a character when no other characters are present. The conventions regarding soliloquies include: they reflect a character's innermost thoughts; the character is addressing the audience. They function a bit like the Chorus in Athenian drama and a bit like voice-overs in television and film. If a character delivers a soliloquy, the convention is that the character believes what s/he is saying—s/he may be lying to him- or herself, but s/he doesn't realize it.

"To be or not to be"

The status of Hamlet's most famous speech is tricky. If Hamlet knows (or even suspects) that Claudius and Polonius (or their agents) are spying on him, this is a monologue that pretends to be a soliloquy, and its representation of Hamlet's "inner thoughts" is a matter of performance over revelation—seeming over being. If Hamlet doesn't know (or suspect) that spies are present, this is apparently a soliloquy that is nonetheless technically a monologue; it can by convention be taken as Hamlet's true inner thoughts. Given events in the play prior to III.i, when this speech occurs, if Hamlet doesn't expect spies everywhere, he must be crazy. (Aye, there's the rub.) Hamlet is not an idiot; is he truly crazy? This one gets played both ways, especially in film versions. Kenneth Branagh's version is a monologue; he is aware of Claudius's and Polonius's presence (he faces a mirror and his eyes dart to the curtained alcove behind him at various points in his delivery). David Tennant's, however, is delivered as a true soliloquy—a confession of innermost thoughts.

If "To be or not to be" is a soliloquy, Hamlet is contemplating suicide very seriously indeed; if it's a monologue, the possibilities are endless—as are the double meanings for his probable auditors: Hamlet may want Claudius to think he's suicidal, but the words "grunt and sweat" and even "to die" (a French euphemism for orgasm) take on an earthier meaning given Polonius's diagnosis that Hamlet is mad with love (*i.e.*, crazy with lust) for Ophelia. Whether Hamlet suspects spies—and their identities—is a decision for actors and directors and readers.

Variant (Multiple Speakers):

Stichomythia: A fairly frequent form of dialogue in which multiple characters share the ten syllables of the standard Shakespearean line, indicated by the second speaker's line starting in the middle of the page rather than at the usual left-hand margin. The effect of such moments is rapid-fire; this dialogic form has a specific page layout that indicates that the actors should not pause between each other's lines. Stichomythia is usually reserved for moments of extreme emotional intensity and urgency (anger; excitement) and/or high tension moments (key plot moments).

Stichomythia is easy to spot visually because of its unique page layout.

Hamlet:	This bad begins and worse remains behind.
	One word more, good lady.
Gertrude:	What shall I do?
Hamlet:	Not this by no means that I bid you do [&c.]

(III.iv.186-88)

Hamlet and Gertrude share line 187; together they speak a full ten-syllable line. The stichomythia here indicates Gertrude's tremendous urgency (and perhaps panic; Hamlet has just killed Polonius and forced her to confront her own betrayal as a mother).

(See Caesura, below, for comparison.)

BASELINE SCENE ENDING: RHYMING COUPLET

In blank verse, two adjacent lines that rhyme comprise a rhyming couplet. Often used to indicate scene endings as it provides an aural cue to the actors waiting to come on stage to begin the next scene. It functions as a bit of a "button" to the scene, as well. Example: "More relative than this. The play's the thing/ Wherein I'll catch the conscience of the King" (II.ii.605-6). (There are other times

Shakespeare uses rhyming couplets; these are generally easy to spot and their function to deduce from context.) Pronunciation has changed since the Elizabethan era; some rhyming couplets now sound less exact than they did to the original groundlings.

IRONY

Shakespeare frequently capitalizes on the possibilities of dramatic irony (not to be confused with irony or situational irony, definitions of which are provided here to clarify the distinctions). Dramatic irony is often used to intensify an audience's emotional response to a situation; it also gratifies the audience's egos by including them "in the know."

Irony: When the words spoken are the literal opposite of the speaker's meaning.

Dramatic Irony: This occurs when the audience knows something a character or group of characters doesn't. Can also occur when some but not all characters on stage share the audience's knowledge. Example: The moment in a horror movie when the audience thinks, "Don't go outside!"

Situational Irony: When events result which are the opposite of what was intended or expected.

STAGE DIRECTION

Most stage directions in current editions are not original to Shakespeare but are editorial suggestions, often indicated by italics or brackets. (Shakespeare's most famous original stage direction is from *The Winter's Tale*: Exit, pursued by a bear [III.iii.57].)

Line Rubric: Stage direction provided in a character's line(s).

Gertrude: Here, Hamlet, take my napkin, rub thy brows.

(V.ii.290)

Language: Concepts, Terms, and Features

BASELINE GENRE: BLANK VERSE

Blank verse, a poetic form defined as "unrhymed iambic pentameter," forms the baseline of Shakespeare's dramatic language. Although the language doesn't strictly adhere to this (endless unvaried iambic pentameter would get boring quickly), this is the standard from which students of Shakespeare's language measure departures and variants.

Baseline Metric (Rhythmic) Pattern—Iambic Pentameter: The baseline metric pattern for Shakespeare's plays is iambic pentameter: ten-syllable lines consisting of five iambs. (Iambs are two syllables; "penta-" = five; 2 x 5 = 10). Given that an iamb contains an unstressed syllable (u) followed by a stressed syllable (/), the rhythm (meter) of a line of iambic pentameter is:

u / u / u / u / u /

The name "Marie" is an iamb; say the name aloud five times ("Marie Marie Marie Marie Marie") to hear the rhythmic (metric) pattern of iambic pentameter.

There are two kinds of variants for blank verse. One is a shift in genre (to another form of metric poetry or to prose); the other kind involves smaller metric variants, called "substitutions."

Genre Variants:

Iambic Tetrameter is the metric pattern used in Shakespeare by witches, elementals, fairies (sometimes), and other supernatural creatures; also, in songs, no matter who is singing them. An iambic tetrameter line contains eight syllables comprised of four iambs. (Iambs are two syllables; "tetra-" = four; 2 x 4 = 8). Given that an iamb contains an unstressed syllable (u) followed by a stressed syllable (/), the rhythm (meter) of a line of iambic tetrameter is:

u / u / u / u /

Say the name "Marie" (an iamb) the name aloud four times to hear the metric pattern of iambic tetrameter. Examples: "A foolish thing was but a toy" (Feste's song, *Twelfth Night* [V.i.391]); "Full fathom five thy father lies" (Ariel's song, *The Tempest* [I.ii.400]).

Prose: Self-explanatory; evident by an even right-hand margin. If Shakespearean characters are speaking in prose, generally one of three things is happening:

    1. There are only lower-class characters on-stage

    2. The character speaking in prose is insane…

    3. … or pretending to be.

Good friends in the upper classes (*e.g.*, Hamlet and Horatio) will sometimes (rarely) switch into prose when they are alone.

LINE ENDINGS (FORMAL VARIATIONS)

End-stopped line: A line of verse that ends with a comma, period, or other punctuation. Can indicate several things—emotional intensity; that a character is unsettled by something; that a character is talking down to someone. It usually indicates either that a usually eloquent and/or intelligent character is temporarily destabilized or that the character might not be very eloquent generally—compare to the character's lines elsewhere in the play to establish which. *(See also: Enjambment.)*

Enjambment/Enjambed: When a line of verse does not end with a comma, period, or other punctuation but continues directly into the next line, these lines are said to be "enjambed." Characters whose lines display consistent frequent enjambment throughout an entire play are generally considered extremely intelligent. The opposite is not necessarily true; lack of enjambment does not necessarily mean that a character is unintelligent.

Metric Variants: Not 10 syllables—Fewer? More?

Caesura: In blank verse, when a line has fewer than ten syllables and is not followed by a stichomythic response (the next speaker's line beginning, instead, at the left margin), the resultant beat or two of silence is called a "caesura." Something happens in every caesura; it's up to the reader/actor/director to figure out and/or decide what that is (or sometimes must be; *see above, Line Rubric*). The more syllables missing (to complete the line's ten), the longer the pause.

> Hamlet: 'Tis heavy with him. And am I then revenged,
> To take him in the purging of his soul,
> When he is fit and seasoned for his passage?
> No!
> Up, sword, and know thou a more horrid hent.
> (III.iii.84-88)

At line 87, Hamlet speaks only one syllable ("No!"); in the caesura that follows, he realizes his shocking decision (and commits a deadly sin; more on that in the section on Act III)—that he is not yet going to do the thing he has waited to do since Act I, the thing he finally has both the justification and opportunity to do: kill Claudius.

Feminine Ending: In blank verse, a line having eleven syllables with the final syllable unstressed is said to have a "feminine ending." Gender equity issues aside (the term is fairly old), lines with feminine endings indicate that some weakness is lurking in the vicinity of the line. Whether the character is identifying a weakness in him- or herself, in what he or she is talking about, in his or her present situation, or in a concept at play in the line varies and depends on denotative meaning and dramatic context. The unstressed eleventh syllable is a clue to the reader/actor to consider how "weakness" may be at play in that particular word, line, or moment.

Extra syllables: Very rarely, a Shakespearean verse line will have a stressed eleventh syllable or more than eleven syllables. This indicates something particularly extreme; what that may be depends on denotative meaning and context. Generally speaking, the more extra syllables there are, the greater the extremity in the character's emotions or situation.

Line Endings: Extended Example

Macbeth: Tomorrow, and tomorrow, and tomorrow
Creeps in this petty pace from day to day
To the last syllable of recorded time,
And all our yesterdays have lighted fools
The way to dusty death. Out, out, brief candle!
Life's but a walking shadow, a poor player
That struts and frets his hour upon the stage
And then is heard no more. It is a tale
Told by an idiot, full of sound and fury,
Signifying nothing.

(*Macbeth*, V.v.19-28)

Macbeth has just learned that his wife has died; she has ever been the stronger partner and was the motivating and intellectual force behind the political decisions that comprise the plot and Macbeth's inner personal tragedy.

Here is the same soliloquy with emphasis added: italics added to indicate feminine endings, bold syllables indicating stresses in strict iambic pentameter, bold/italics marking extra syllables in the twelve-syllable line, and a bracketed ellipsis marking the caesura.

Macbeth: *Tomorrow, and tomorrow, and tomorrow*
Creeps in this petty pace from day to day
To the last syllable of recorded time,
And all our yesterdays have lighted fools
The way to dusty death. Out, out, brief candle!
Life's but a walking shadow, a poor player
That **struts** and **frets** his **hour** upon the **stage**
And then is heard no more. It is a tale
Told by an idiot, full of sound and ***fury,***

> Signifying nothing. [...]

Exploring the exceptional lines in this soliloquy in order might yield this:

Feminine endings: The soliloquy has four lines with feminine endings, which first alternate and then are juxtaposed. The presence of feminine endings is an indication of some weakness lurking about (whether in situation or speaker or perspective or judgment depends on context).

> *Tomorrow, and tomorrow, and tomorrow*

From Macbeth's perspective, tomorrow is weaker than yesterday; his wife has just died, and he faces the future without her.

> *To the last syllable of recorded time,*

Time with her was strong; time without her is weak. Macbeth faces an eternity of time without his wife; time without her is empty compared to time with her.

> *The way to dusty death. Out, out, brief candle!*

Her life is the candle. It is over. A candle flame is weak; her life, finally measured, was weak. She is dead because of their weaknesses, and he knows it.

> *Life's but a walking shadow, a poor player*

Macbeth compares life to a bad (and perhaps pitiable) actor. Life feels weak, not-real; here he moves past the painful thoughts of tomorrow and casts his despair retrospectively over their lives particularly and all of life in general.

Strict iambic pentameter:

> That **struts** and **frets** his **hour** upon the **stage**

In the very next line, Macbeth shifts abruptly to strict iambic pentameter, a metric pattern that often indicates what the speaker thinks is usual, ordinary, or normal; perhaps what "should be."

Macbeth's metric shift conveys his bleak view of life—that it is nothing more than going through the motions according to the rules.

Extra syllables:

Told by an idiot, full of sound and *fury,*

Macbeth is losing control—his emotions are overwhelming him, reflected by the language escaping the "control" of the ten-syllable line with the evocative word "fury." Fury can mean several things; as Shakespeare has added it as an entire extra foot, this is a fantastic place to pause and consider its many definitions and how they might be at play in context. One definition of fury is "frenetic yet pointless activity," which fits the tenor of this soliloquy. Another is "anger past the point of reason," which might indicate that Macbeth will soon explode into rage and furious action. At least a double meaning is probable here.

Caesura:

Signifying nothing. [...]

The six-syllable line in "signifying nothing" requires a caesura, or silence, which seems especially strong here, as it allows the word "nothing" to echo in "nothingness." Not only is this a profound statement of despair, its silent echo subtly hearkens back to the audible echoes of "tomorrow" in the first line. Macbeth's despair is circular; it is a closed system from which he can find no escape save through death.

SCANSION

The inexact art and science of metric analysis whereby substitutions are identified and possible variants are explored is called "scansion" or "scanning."

Metric Variants: Substitutions

When a line is not in strict iambic pentameter (five disyllabic iambic "feet" or two-syllable parts), any metric foot that is not an iamb is called a "substitution."

Scansion and substitution are best illustrated by example.

Scansion and Substitution: Example #1

The stressed syllables are rendered in bold:

Richard: **Now** is | the **win**|ter of | our **dis** | content

(*Richard III*, I.i.1)

In this example...

... the first "foot" ("**Now** is") is a substitution: a trochee (/ u) substituted for iamb.

... the second ("the **win**-"), fourth ("our **dis**-"), and fifth ("con**tent**") feet are iambs (u /)—the "baseline" foot.

... the third "foot" ("-ter of") is also a substitution: pyrrhus (u u) substituted for iamb.

Substitutions are "exceptional," that is, exceptions to the rule; they vary the "baseline" meter in ways that are audible. Although ten syllables pass very quickly on stage, substitutions provide actors with clues for where to consider the language more closely. What might it mean, for example, for a character to begin a play with a substitution? What might this say about his character's regard for rules, with the law, with God's law? And why the emphasis on the word "Now"? In the remainder of the soliloquy, Richard describes "Now," delves briefly into the recent past, and then outlines his own villainous plans for the future. So the play starts with the "now," but what is "now" is ephemeral, turning to dust under Richard's machinations.

Scansion and Substitution: Example #2

Ophelia: Oh, what a noble mind is here o'erthrown!

(*Hamlet*, III.i.153)

There are several ways to scan this line, and it's up to the reader, the actor, the director—it depends on what sort of nuance you want to add:

Ophelia A: Oh, **what** a **no**ble **mind** is **here** o'er**thrown**!

Strict iambic pentameter, lamenting the loss of Hamlet's once-ordered mind—a perfectly valid choice for this character.

Ophelia B: **Oh, what** a **no**ble **mind is here o'erthrown**!

Here, the first, fourth, and fifth feet are given extra stress (called "spondees"; *see page 37*). This delivery choice portrays an overwrought Ophelia—also a perfectly valid choice for this character in this moment.

Ophelia A is upset but not overwrought; perhaps she's too shocked to emote just yet. Ophelia B is overwrought, perhaps by anger; perhaps by despair. Scansion choices do not foreclose emotional ones; scansion is but one tool for the actor.

Scansion and Substitution: Example #3

Juliet: My only love sprung from my only hate!

(*Romeo and Juliet*, I.v.139)

Juliet's line can be scanned (and thus delivered) several ways; two examples follow:

Juliet A: My **only love sprung** from my **only hate**!

By starting her line with an iamb, Juliet A emphasizes the word "only"—a fitting choice given that Romeo is her first love (and will be her only love).

Juliet B: **My** only **love sprung** from my **only hate**!

By stressing both syllables in the first foot (replacing the iamb with a spondee; *see below*), Juliet B emphasizes the word "My." This scansion provides a different nuance; that emphasis reinforces the line's denotative content, which punctuates the shift of Juliet's loyalty from her family to herself and her love for Romeo.

Both choices are valid (and there are several others). An actor might switch this out from performance to performance; slight variations are one way to keep a performance fresh.

METRIC FEET (SELECTED)

u = unstressed syllable, / = stressed syllable

Disyllables (feet with two syllables)

Iamb (iambic): Baseline Foot: (u /) The word "until" is iambic.

Pyrrhus (pyrrhic): (u u) Pyrrhic feet usually occur when two unstressed syllables from longer polysyllabic words occur in a line such that they comprise a foot in themselves. Example: The middle two syllables of "always between" could comprise a pyrrhic foot:

al- |ways be- | **tween**.

Trochee (trochaic): (/ u) The name "Alice" is trochaic.

Spondee (spondaic): (/ /) A disyllabic metric foot containing a double stress. Any two-syllable name shouted to get someone's attention (*e.g.*, "STELLA!") is spondaic.

Trisyllables (feet with three syllables)

Because the standard foot in blank verse is a disyllable (iamb), trisyllabic substitutions are fairly rare in Shakespeare's plays, usually occurring at exceptional line-ends.

Tribrach (tribrachic): (u u u) Very rare; usually occurs when three unstressed syllables of two adjacent words comprise a single foot.

Dactyl (dactylic): (/ u u) "Dactyl" is from the Greek word for for "finger"; the stress pattern mimics the distances between finger joints (long, short, short). The word "anyway" is dactylic.

Amphibrach (amphibrachic): (u / u) The name "Joanna" is an amphibrach; the amphibrachs are the first two feet in the opening line of a limerick ("There once was | a stone in | my shoe.")

Anapest (anapestic): (u u /) The word "afternoon" is an anapest.

Bacchius (bacchic): (u / /) Bacchic feet are often amphibrachic feet with different emphasis. The word "martini" can be both bacchic (mar**ti**ni) and amphibrachic (mar**ti**ni).

Cretic (cretic): (/ u /) The command "Go away" is cretic.

Molossus (molossic): (/ / /) Any three-syllable name shouted to get someone's attention (*e.g.*, "EMILY!") is molossic

Aurality: Concepts, Terms, and Features

AURAL DEVICES

Alliteration (alliterative): Repeated consonant sounds.

Assonance (assonant): Repeated vowel sounds.

Onomatopoeia (onomatopoeic): A word that sounds like what it is (*e.g.*, crunch, smash, shatter, etc.).

Aural Devices: Example

The use of aural devices isn't limited to Shakespeare or even so-called "literary" works; contemporary mystery writer Donna Leon uses aural devices to great effect in the following example (from 2009):

"Patches of the domes poked through the snow, which Brunetti could see was beginning to melt in the morning sun. Saints popped up from everywhere, a lion flew by, boats hooted at one another, and Brunetti closed his eyes from the joy of it."

(About Face, 176-77)

Alliteration: patches, poked, popped up (p); snow, see; sun, saints (s); melt, morning (m); by, boats (b); closed, his, eyes (z).

Assonance: domes, poked, snow (long o); up, from (short u); one, another (short u).

Onomatopoeia: popped up; hooted. You could make an argument for "poked" and the combination of "melt" and "morning," as well.

Antithesis (antithetical): A syntactically exact compressed playing off of opposites, creating an echo effect, inviting readers to compare parallel words. The longer the antithetical elements, the less exact the syntactic echo need be.

Antithesis: Example #1 (Syntactically Exact)

Gertrude: Hamlet, thou hast thy father much offended.

Hamlet: Mother, you have my father much offended.

(Hamlet, III.iv.10-11)

The lines are antithetical and the syntactic echo is exact:

Gertrude: [address][informal pron.][verb][poss. pron.][adv.][adj.]

Hamlet: [address][formal pron.] [verb][poss. pron.][adv.][adj.]

The "opposites" are subtle—Hamlet sets "Mother" up in opposition to himself ("Hamlet") and changes the second-person pronoun from informal ("thou") to the formal ("you"). Subtle but powerful. Hamlet is furious, and this III.iv confrontation has been coming since I.ii (and building for months before that).

Antithesis: Example #2 (Syntactically Inexact)

Richard: Never came poison from so sweet a place.

Anne: Never hung poison on a fouler toad.

(Richard III, II.i.146-147)

The syntax isn't exact, but it's close enough for an echo effect:

Richard: [adv.][verb][noun][prep.][adv.][adj.][article][noun].

Anne: [adv.][verb][noun][prep.]   [article][adj.][noun].

The opposition is less subtle (and these two verbal combatants less evenly matched, perhaps): the "sweet place" is Anne's lips (she has just spit at Richard); the opposition is the "toad" (Richard). Ironically, this princess will kiss (marry) this frog. It will, predictably, not go well.

Poetic Contraction: A contraction made when omitting a syllable to preserve meter. Example: "O'er" for "over."

Rhyme:

> **Exact rhyme**: Self-explanatory—the rhyme is exact: cat/hat; through/blue.

> **Near rhyme**: Also self-explanatory—the rhyme is close, but not exact: mourn/before. Near rhymes depend on assonance.

> **Internal rhyme**: When a rhyme occurs not at the end of a line but somewhere in the middle, it's called an internal rhyme.

FIGURATIVE LANGUAGE

Metaphor (metaphorical): A comparison drawn without using "like" or "as."

> **Conceit**: An extended metaphor (*e.g., Richard III*'s opening soliloquy draws an extended conceit using musical terms whereby his definition of "peace" becomes "a dance").

Simile: A comparison drawn using "like" or "as."

Part II

Study Guide
and Questions

A General Introduction to *Hamlet*

THE TRAGEDY OF *Hamlet* overtly concerns love versus duty; in almost every scene in which Hamlet appears, something he loves (or wants to do, motivated from within) comes into direct conflict with his duty (something he must do, imposed from without—or sometimes imposed from within him out of a sense of responsibility to more than just himself). This will take many forms—only his relationship with his best friend Horatio is untouched by this tragic dilemma.

Horatio provides a bit of the political context in the opening scene, but because he speaks—at least in that moment—in a very erudite manner, and because the moment goes by very quickly, here is that context:

Denmark/Norway

The Denmark/Norway political situation is tense and convoluted when the play begins. At some time in the past, the King of Denmark (Hamlet, Sr., Hamlet's father, also called "Denmark") and the King of Norway (Fortinbras, Sr., also called "Norway") had a "Devil Went Down to Georgia" kind of challenge: they bet sections of their countries' land on the outcome of a contest of arms ("I think I'm better'n you"). Whoever won got to keep their own land, obviously, and also got a part of the other country. Denmark (Hamlet, Sr.) won.

Both of these kings are now dead, and in both cases, the crown passed to their brothers (Claudius in Denmark; Fortinbras, Sr.'s brother in Norway). This doesn't mean the crown was stolen from the sons; at least in *Hamlet*, neither country inherits according to primogeniture, in which the first-born son inherits. In *Hamlet*, Denmark and Norway instead follow a system called "tanistry" in which a King selects and names his heir—not necessarily his first-born son—from amongst his male relatives. This system would have been known to Shakespeare's audience; Scottish and other Celtic clans choose their chiefs by tanistry. During Shakespeare's era, Scotland especially would have been very much on Londoners' minds, as Elizabeth I was too old to bear children, and her heir was James VI of Scotland (son of Mary, Queen of Scots).

One question that arises here is "So why didn't Hamlet, Sr., name his son Hamlet, Jr., as his heir?" and another is "Did he really name his brother, Claudius, as his heir?" Since Hamlet, Jr., was away at college when his father died, one possibility is that Hamlet, Sr., had selected Claudius, intending to change that as soon as Hamlet, Jr., finished his education. Another possibility is that Claudius is lying about the whole thing. Can you figure this out from the play? Something to keep an eye on.

Young Fortinbras is the son of the former Norwegian king (and nephew to the current king), much like Hamlet is the son of the former Danish king (and nephew to the current king).

Fortinbras, Jr., without his uncle the King's knowledge, is raising armies, determined to take back that part of Norway his father gambled and lost. This is in defiance of the law (duty) but it does make a kind of emotional sense (love). (The love/duty conflict is everywhere.)

Foil Relationship: The Royal Houses of Denmark and Norway

The foil relationship between the family trees of the royal houses of Norway and Denmark are exact in all ways save one—no mother/wife is mentioned for Norway, but we do meet Denmark's: Gertrude (Hamlet's mother/former queen/current queen). Every time a foil relationship contains a difference, pay wicked close attention to it; it's important. So pay close attention to Gertrude. She's a total wild card in this play and poses some questions that the text does not answer anywhere. (She has nothing to do with Claudius's claim to the throne, by the way; their marriage in no way cements his political power; dowager queens are just dowager queens, not ruling queens. He gets nothing but a wife—and some problems—by marrying her, so it's not a political marriage.)

Another important foil relationship between these houses occurs with the characters of Hamlet, Jr., and Fortinbras, Jr. (No, it's not subtle. Foil relationships are often obvious, but you can nonetheless learn a great deal that's very nuanced from paying close attention to them.)

Hamlet's Character

Some people say that Hamlet suffers from procrastination and indecision; it goes deeper than that, though, and touches on a larger division that colored much of the Renaissance. He does seem to take a very long time to make up his mind about things until you spot that he's setting up a logic problem and refuses to act until he has sufficient evidence for action (which occurs in III.ii, at the "turn"). After that, things still take a long time, but we'll talk about that when we get there; this is one of those plays that pivots neatly in the middle and becomes someone else's play for most of the second half. The first half of the play asks and answers the question "What will Hamlet do?"; the second half asks and answers the question "What will Claudius do?" (and, depending on how you read her character, "What will Gertrude do?").

If this is your first time reading the play, see what you notice.

If you've read the play several times already and are looking to go deeper in a historical or cultural way, here's something additional to think about: Although Hamlet's personal tragedy is a question of love versus duty, the larger philosophical, political, and theological dilemma is one of faith versus works as the path to Christian Heaven. The "faith versus works" debate drove much of the major political trauma of the Renaissance, from the crisis of church and state in France to the six marriages of Henry VIII to the Protestant revolution/Reformation (depending on which side you're on). A big clue that the play engages this debate is Hamlet's university, Wittenberg, where Martin Luther taught Theology (*i.e.,* Philosophy). "Faith versus works" is a recurring subtext throughout this play. *(See Introduction, pages 9-12.)*

Characters

BECAUSE THE PLAY forwards such ambiguity regarding many of these characters, this section will address only such vital statistics as aren't obvious (*e.g.*, that Horatio is not a citizen of Denmark and thus owes no political fealty or blind obedience to either Claudius or Hamlet; that Hamlet was not the named heir to his father's throne). This section focuses rather on the ambiguities and questions with which readers, actors, and directors must engage as they work to understand each character at any given moment in the play. The questions herein are not proscriptive; they are offered as possible starting points for further exploration.

Larger issues, concepts, dualities, and stakes of the play considered in this section include:

Seeming/Being (Appearance/Reality)

Ways of Knowing (Epistemology; Methodology)

Spying (witnessing)/Logic (*a.k.a.*, philosophy; propositional logic)

Love/Duty

Faith/Works

Madness/Reason

Suicide

Disease/Poison/Rot/Decay (literal and figurative)

Characters appear alphabetically for ease of reference. Identifying tags occurring after character names are from the *Dramatis Personae* given in Bevington and Kastan's *Four Tragedies* (46-7), to which this guide is keyed.

Characters

Ambassador *(See First Ambassador)*

Bernardo, officer; soldier on watch

To what extent is he operating out of love or duty in any given context and moment?

When and to what extent is his personality distinguishable from Francisco's? Marcellus's? To what dramatic objective?

When and to what extent is he operating as part of a collective? To what dramatic objective?

How does Bernardo serve as a possible foil for his companions of the watch (Francisco and Marcellus)? Toward what end?

How does the collective comprised of Bernardo, Francisco, and Marcellus serve as a suggestive foil for other collectives in the play (*e.g.*, Cornelius and Voltimand; Rosencrantz and Guildenstern; Hamlet and Horatio; the Players, etc.)? Toward what end?

Captain in Fortinbras's army

How does the Captain serve as a possible foil for other messengers in the play (*e.g.*, Cornelius and Voltimand, Rosencrantz and Guildenstern, the First Ambassador, possibly even the Ghost)? Toward what end?

How does the Captain serve as a possible foil for other soldiers in the play (*e.g.*, Bernardo, Francisco, and Marcellus; possibly the Ghost; possibly Hamlet, in his role as Prince)? Toward what end?

Claudius, King of Denmark, the former King's brother

Although Claudius achieved the throne through murder, when the play opens he is, as far as anyone knows, legally King, having presumably been publicly named heir by his late brother. *(See Hamlet.)*

Claudius's claim to the throne has nothing to do with marrying Gertrude. She was wife, not hereditary heir; marrying her does not stabilize his power in any way—if anything, it risked doing the opposite, as this marriage was legally considered incestuous (at the time, the law drew no distinction between sisters and sisters-in-law).

When he uses the word "we" it is often in its usage as "the royal we"—the convention that ruling monarchs refer to themselves in the plural, reflecting their doubled identity as monarch and the State. This occasionally blurs with Claudius; sometimes his use of "we" seems also or instead to refer to himself and Gertrude.

It is interesting that Claudius's name, like Cornelius's, is Latinate; if there is a Germanic-derived paired character name, it is interesting to consider whose name(s) might complete the pair.

If you find it impossible to feel any sympathy for Claudius, watch Patrick Stewart's brilliant and heartbreaking (yet chilling) delivery of the III.iii soliloquy (available on YouTube).

As Claudius is an obvious foil for Hamlet (for they must be somewhat evenly matched in power, if not in kind of power) for the play to achieve necessary tension, many (but not all) of the questions that surround and drive Hamlet's character also surround and drive Claudius's.

Character questions:

To what extent might Claudius be considered a tragic character in his own right? *(See **Hamlet, Gertrude, Ophelia**.)*

In any given context and moment...

... to what extent is he seeming and/or acting authentically ("being")?

... on whom is he spying?

... who is spying on him?

... to what extent is he motivated by love and/or duty?

... to what extent is he embodying the concept faith and/or that of "works"?

... to what extent is he motivated by his feelings for and about Gertrude?

... power?

... ambition?

... fear?

... his role as King of Denmark?

... his identity as a murderer?

... a position of political superiority?

... desperation?

When he uses "we," is he referring to himself in the royal plural? Or to himself and Gertrude? Both? Are there times this is clear and times when it is murky? When? To what end?

To what degree and in what instances does he rely on propositional logic? Toward what end?

To what degree and in what instances does he rely on other ways of knowing? Toward what end?

How is he an unlikely but arguably perhaps the best foil for Hamlet?

When and to what extent might he serve as a suggestive foil for other characters (*e.g.*, the Ghost, Norway, Polonius)?

When and to what extent might he and Hamlet, as a pair, benefit from comparison to other paired characters (*e.g.*, Cornelius and

Voltimand; Rosencrantz and Guildenstern; Polonius and Laertes; the Ghost and Hamlet; Gertrude and Hamlet)?

And, in every instance, how? Why? Toward what end?

Clowns (a gravedigger and his companion)

What commentary do the Clowns provide on any of the play's larger issues, binaries, and stakes? Love and duty? Faith and works? Insanity? Suicide? Seeming versus being?

Do the Clowns deploy propositional logic? Toward what end? Do they use the method well or is their use somehow flawed?

Do the Clowns have distinguishable personalities? How so? Toward what end?

How do the Clowns serve as possible foils for each other? Toward what end?

Does either of the Clowns serve as a possible foil for other characters in the play (*e.g.*, Marcellus; the Priest)? Who? How? Toward what end?

How does this pair serve as a suggestive foil for other pairs in the play (*e.g.*, Rosencrantz and Guildenstern; Hamlet and Horatio; Cornelius and Voltimand; etc.)? Toward what end?

What dramatic purpose does this pair serve?

What earlier moment(s) does their single scene echo?

Cornelius and **Voltimand**, members of the Danish court

Very, very minor characters whose shared first line, "In that, and all things, will we show our duty" (I.ii.40), nonetheless encapsulates the play's larger stakes in microcosm: the question of duty and ways of knowing/the method of propositional logic. Carrying a message to the King of Norway to ascertain whether Norway and Denmark were actually at war was a life or death proposition; they are pawns in Claudius's propositional logic:

IF the King of Norway approves his nephew's invasion of Denmark,

THEN he may very well send back Cornelius and Voltimand's heads;

THEN I shall know,

THEREFORE, we are at war.

There are no throw-away lines in Shakespeare.

Their names are Latinate and Germanic, respectively; this underscores the play's nod toward the Catholic/Protestant schism represented more obviously in the names Rosencrantz and Guildenstern and gestures toward the larger issue of faith versus works (love and duty by any other name; see *Introduction, pp. 7-12*). Voltimand's name is particularly evocative, homonymically suggesting some etymological derivation from "flight of hand" ("vol de main" in French)—an excellent name for a messenger; a suggestive name to connect to "works."

Character questions:

Are their personalities separable? When, and to what extent? In either case, to what dramatic objective?

How does this pair serve as a suggestive foil for other pairs in the play (*e.g.,* Rosencrantz and Guildenstern; Hamlet and Horatio; the Clowns; etc.)? Toward what end?

How does this pair serve as a suggestive foil for other messengers in the play (*e.g.,* the Captain, the First Ambassador, perhaps Gertrude [*viz.* Ophelia's death], perhaps the Ghost)?

How does this pair's function serve as a suggestive foil for other instances of propositional logic in the play?

Denmark (when used as a name): Refers to the past or present King of Denmark.

England (when used as a name): Refers to the present King of England.

First Ambassador from England

How does the First Ambassador serve as a suggestive foil for other messengers in the play (*e.g.*, the Captain, Cornelius and Voltimand, perhaps Gertrude [*viz.* Ophelia's death], perhaps the Ghost)?

What propositional logic statement is resolved with his appearance in V.ii? To what dramatic end?

To what extent does his appearance in V.ii provide a bookend echo of the Ghost's appearance in I.i?

Fortinbras, Prince of Norway

Like Hamlet (Jr.), Fortinbras (Jr.) is a Prince bent on exacting revenge for his father's death, although his own father's death did not stem from a crime—it occurred as part of a legal contest-at-arms. He is an obvious foil for Hamlet; considering the particulars of their foil relationship provides an excellent introduction to foil relationships and their purposes generally. His name is Latinate, deriving etymologically from "fort en bras"—"strong in arm(s)."

Francisco, officer; soldier on watch

To what extent is he operating out of love or duty in any given context and moment?

When and to what extent is his personality distinguishable from Bernardo's? Marcellus's? To what dramatic objective?

When and to what extent is he operating as part of a collective? To what dramatic objective?

How does Francisco serve as a possible foil for his companions of the watch (Bernardo and Marcellus)? Toward what end?

How does the collective comprised of Bernardo, Francisco, and Marcellus serve as a suggestive foil for other collectives in the play (*e.g.*, Cornelius and Voltimand; Rosencrantz and Guildenstern; Hamlet and Horatio; the Players, etc.)? Toward what end?

Gertrude, Queen of Denmark, widow of the former King and now wife of Claudius

The character of Gertrude comprises the play's central ambiguity, an ambiguity it does not resolve. The absence of resolution is itself fasinating. This ambiguity is identified and addressed in the character questions that follow. (*See also the Introduction, p. 4.*)

Character questions:

Does she have any idea that Claudius murdered her late husband?

If so, for how much (if any) of the play has she known?

Was she in on it from the beginning or does she realize it during the course of the play?

If the latter, when?

... and is her realization the work of an instant, or a growing suspicion?

If the latter, does she receive confirmation of that suspicion? When?

If not, why not?

To what extent (and from what point in the play) might Gertrude be considered a tragic character in her own right? (*See **Claudius, Hamlet, Ophelia**.*)

When is she motivated by love? Duty? Both? To what extent does she consciously realize either?

To what extent is she intellectually savvy (or politically savvy) enough to understand the intricacies of her son's double meanings?

Does she ever deploy propositional logic? When? Toward what end?

Does she know that the cup contains poison?

… or suspect?

Ophelia is an obvious foil for Gertrude; are there others? Who? Toward what end?

Is there anyone who cannot be considered a foil for Gertrude? Who? Toward what end?

As always, how, when, and why?

The Ghost of Hamlet, former King of Denmark

The identity of the Ghost is the central question Hamlet must answer in the first half of the play: Is this truly the Ghost of his father (in which case he must kill Claudius)? Or is it a demon sent to tempt him into sacrificing his immortal soul (in which case he must not kill Claudius)? Because Hamlet cannot trust the evidence of his eyes regarding the Ghost's identity, he embarks on a series of propositional logic statements which do not resolve until III.ii—when, ironically, he achieves visual evidence of Claudius's guilt, thereby realizing the limits of propositional logic in service of theological questions.

The play answers the central question of the Ghost, but others remain.

Character questions:

To what extent does the Ghost ask the impossible of Hamlet? By what right?

Was the Ghost the good King, husband, and father of Hamlet's memory? What evidence exists in support of and/or in contradiction to Hamlet's memories?

What makes a good King, husband, and father?

To what extent might the Ghost serve as a suggestive foil to other characters (*e.g.*, Hamlet, Claudius, the late Fortinbras [Sr.], Polonius, Gertrude)?

To what extent might the Ghost and Hamlet, considered together, serve as a suggestive foil pair for other pairs in the play, (*e.g.*, Claudius and Hamlet, Gertrude and Hamlet, Fortinbras [Sr. and Jr.], Polonius and Laertes, any authority figure over any subordinate)?

To what extent does the Ghost embody (or seem to embody) the play's larger issues, dualities, and ambiguities (*e.g.*, love/duty, faith/works, seeming/being, madness, poison/disease, spying, etc.)?

Gravedigger *(See **Clowns**)*

Guildenstern, member of the Danish court *(See **Rosencrantz and Guildenstern**)*

Hamlet, Prince of Denmark, son of the late King and Gertrude

Hamlet is not legally King when the play begins. He is named as Claudius's heir in I.ii; he was not, however, named his father's— Claudius was. For Claudius to have assumed the throne without having been publicly named his brother's legal heir would have been obvious treason, and although Claudius will bend the law to marry Gertrude (for which he thanks the court in I.ii), obvious treason seems highly, highly unlikely. It is therefore nearly certain that Hamlet, Sr., named Claudius his heir—albeit perhaps only as a placeholder until Hamlet, Jr., completed his studies abroad. Once Hamlet learns that Claudius achieved the throne via murder, the mantle of moral and rightful Kingship falls on him, and he must be judged (and must judge himself) not only as son but also in his execution of the rightful King's justice. *(See also Introduction, pp. 6-12.)*

Character questions:

In any given context and moment…

… to what extent is he seeming and/or acting authentically ("being")?

… on whom is he spying?

… who is spying on him?

… to what extent is he motivated by love and/or duty?

… to what extent is he embodying the concept faith and/or that of "works"?

… to what extent is he mad (insane) or merely pretending to be?

… to what extent is he actively suicidal or merely examining the idea of suicide from a philosophical and theological position?

… to what extent is he motivated by his feelings for and about his mother?

… his father?

… his stepfather?

… Ophelia?

… his role as Prince and heir to the throne?

… his identity as a student of philosophy?

… a position of superior intellect?

… fear?

To what degree and in what instances does he rely on propositional logic? To what end?

To what degree and in what instances does he rely on other ways of knowing? To what end?

How is every other character in the play a possible foil for Hamlet?

Are there any who aren't?

And, in every instance, how? Why? Toward what end?

Horatio, Hamlet's friend and fellow student

Horatio is not a citizen of Denmark, and thus has no duty to the State of Denmark and owes no political fealty nor blind obedience to Claudius or to Hamlet as Prince. This renders him an excellent point of comparison for other characters.

As his name is Italianate, if a character exists to occupy the Germanic-derived position in an implied pair *(see **Cornelius and***

Voltimand), Hamlet is an obvious choice (although perhaps not the only choice). Something to think about in light of questions of philosophy, ways of knowing, and the limitations thereof...

Character questions:

As Horatio does remarkably little to advance the plot, why might Shakespeare have included Horatio in this play?

What function does he serve in each of his scenes?

How does his presence complicate the questions of madness, suicide, and ways of knowing?

To what extent does Horatio embody the potential and/or the limitations of love, duty, faith, works, philosophy, and reason? How? When?

To what extent might Horatio serve as a suggestive foil for other characters in the play (*e.g.,* Hamlet, Fortinbras, Laertes, Ophelia, Gertrude, the Ghost, Rosencrantz and Guildenstern [considered together as a single character], etc.)?

To what extent might Horatio and Hamlet, considered together, serve as a suggestive foil pair for other pairs in the play (*e.g.,* Claudius and Hamlet; Gertrude and Hamlet; Ophelia and Hamlet; Laertes and Ophelia; Polonius and Claudius; Gertrude and Claudius; any character in a close relationship with any character of relatively greater power; etc.)?

In all cases, how, when, and toward what end?

Laertes, son of Polonius

Laertes is initially presented as an obvious foil for Hamlet in his roles as "son" and also someone who also loves Ophelia (albeit as brother, not romantically)—tracing the development of this foil relationship is a potentially rich avenue for exploration; the extent to which Laertes later serves as a stand-in for Fortinbras, who appears on stage only at the end of Act V, provides an excellent opportunity for considering how drama achieves structural coherence in performance.

Character questions:

On whom does Laertes spy?

By whom is he spied on? When? Toward what end?

To what extent is he an agent or a pawn? When? Why?

To what extent is Laertes motivated by love? Duty? Both? When? How? Toward what end?

Do they always operate in tandem, or are they ever split for this character? When? How? Toward what end?

To what extent does Laertes embody dualities of faith and works, and in what balance?

... madness and reason, and in what balance?

Does Laertes ever deploy propositional logic in service of knowing? When?

If not, what methodology does he deploy?

In addition to Hamlet, to what extent might Laertes serve as a suggestive foil to other characters in the play? Which?

Are there any characters to whom Laertes does not serve as a suggestive foil? Which?

To what extent does Laertes's family (himself, his father, and his sister) serve as a foil for the Royal family of Denmark? Norway?

In all cases, how, when, and toward what end?

Marcellus, officer; soldier on watch

To what extent is he operating out of love or duty in any given context and moment?

When and to what extent is his personality distinguishable from Bernardo's? Francisco's? To what dramatic objective?

When and to what extent is he operating as part of a collective? To what dramatic objective?

How does Marcellus serve as a possible foil for his companions of the watch (Bernardo and Francisco)? Toward what end?

How does the collective comprised of Bernardo, Francisco, and Marcellus serve as a suggestive foil for other collectives in the play (*e.g.*, Cornelius and Voltimand; Rosencrantz and Guildenstern; Hamlet and Horatio; the Players, etc.)? Toward what end?

Norway (when used as a name) Refers to the past or present King of Norway.

Ophelia, daughter of Polonius

The ambiguity presented by Ophelia's character is similar to that proposed by Gertrude's: How much does she know; how much does she figure out; when; what does she do with this knowledge? *(See Introduction, pp. 4-5.)* As such, the play's two female chracters are obvious foils in ways much richer than mere questions of gender and love for Hamlet.

Character questions:

To what extent might Ophelia be considered a tragic character in her own right? *(See **Claudius, Gertrude, Hamlet**.)*

To what extent and when is Ophelia motivated by love? Duty? Both?

Are they in tandem or in conflict for her? When?

To what extent does she embody the play's larger issues, dualities, and stakes (*e.g.*, faith and works, suicide, madness and reason, faithfulness, etc.)? How, when, and toward what end?

What method(s) does Ophelia deploy, if any, as she strives to know?

In addition to Gertrude, to what extent might Ophelia serve as a suggestive foil to other characters in the play? Which?

Are there any characters to whom Ophelia does not serve as a suggestive foil? Which?

To what extent does Ophelia's family (herself, her father, and her brother) serve as a foil for the Royal family of Denmark? Norway?

In all cases, how, when, and toward what end?

Osric, member of the Danish court

Although Osric is a relatively minor character and appears in only one act, his character presents actors and especially directors and choreographers with an ambiguity they must resolve: Is he in on Claudius and Laertes's plan regarding the poisoned, sharpened foils? As fencing match judge, can he not be in on the plan? And what staging decisions and stage business must derive from decisions regarding these ambiguities?

To what extent does Osric serve as a suggestive foil to other characters in the play—as messenger, clown, servant, member of the court, pawn, and embodiment of ambiguity? Why, how, and toward what end?

The Players

The Players' function as meta-commentary on acting and theater, and, in their performance of *The Murder of Gonzago*, on the Royal family of Denmark are interesting to consider and too important to go unnoted here.

Character questions:

How do the Players embody seeming versus being?

To what extent can they be considered exempt from questions of love and duty? Implicated in these questions?

   … faith and works?

… madness and reason?

How does their existence imply commentary on various ways of knowing?

What might it mean that only through their "seeming" does Hamlet learn the authentic, undeniable truth regarding Claudius's guilt?

Polonius, councilor to the King

Polonius's actions are governed by his perfect deployment of propositional logic based on a flawed assumption: that Hamlet's madness is real and stems from one single cause: desire for Ophelia. If one accepts the rhetorical rule of three, in which the last thing listed is the most important, then Polonius unwittingly argues for the foil relationship between Claudius (who lists Gertrude last amongst the three motives behind his crime) and Hamlet (who supposedly abandons reason because of Ophelia). Despite the fact that Polonius's logic is based on a flawed assumption, it does not therefore follow that Hamlet does not love Ophelia; the play is far more interesting (and painful) if his desire for her is as real and sharp as his other emotional dilemmas.

Polonius, as a courtier, cannot ever claim the crown; his goal is to be as close to and as influential on its power as possible. His ambition is as opportunistic as Claudius's; the salient difference is that the means by which he seeks to satisfy it are legal (however morally problematic).

Character questions:

How does Polonius's character fit into, resonate, or comment on the play's dualities and larger stakes (*e.g.*, love and duty, faith and works, ways of knowing, madness and reason, etc.)?

To which other characters might Polonius serve as a suggestive foil (*e.g.*, Claudius, Gertrude [as a parent], Hamlet, Marcellus [who likewise delivers gems of wisdom], other parents, other clowns or comic relief characters)?

To what extent does Polonius play the hero in his own personal narrative?

How and to what extent does Polonius seem (perhaps alone of all characters) to miss the fact that he's acting in a tragedy, mistaking it for a comedy (which conventionally end in weddings)? Toward what end?

Are there any characters to whom Polonius does not serve as a suggestive foil? Which?

To what extent does Polonius's family (himself, his daughter, and his son) serve as a foil for the Royal family of Denmark? Norway?

In all cases, how, when, and toward what end?

The Priest [at Ophelia's funeral]

Does the Priest have a discernible individual personality, or does his character function purely symbolically?

Toward what end might Shakespeare have included a Priest in this play?

Are there any characters to whom the Priest (in personality or symbolic function) might serve a suggestive foil?

What commentary might his presence suggest on the play's larger issues, dualities, and stakes?

Reynaldo, servant to Polonius

Reynaldo is identified as "Polonius's man," which indicates very high (possibly the highest) rank amongst the family's servants.

Character questions:

To what extent does Reynaldo have a discernible personality?

What commentary might his presence suggest on the play's larger issues, dualities, and stakes?

Are there any characters to whom Reynaldo (in personality or symbolic function) might serve a suggestive foil?

Are there any pairs of character to whom the pair Reynaldo and Polonius might serve as a suggestive foil?

In all cases, how, when, and toward what end?

Rosencrantz and **Guildenstern**, members of the Danish court

For an exploration of their names as a homonymic invocation of faith and works duality in this play, see Introduction, pages 7-8.

Are their personalities separable? When, and to what extent? In either case, toward what end?

To what extent are they motivated (individually and/or collectively) by love? Duty? Both? How and when?

Why does Hamlet initially forgive them their status as Claudius's pawns and then turn on them, arguably viciously, definitely fatally? What causes the reversal of Hamlet's position?

How do Rosencrantz and Guildenstern individually (or considered as a single entity) serve as a suggestive foil for other characters in the play (*e.g.*, Horatio)?

How does this pair serve as a suggestive foil for other pairs in the play (*e.g.*, Cornelius and Voltimand; Hamlet and Horatio; the Clowns; etc.)?

How does this pair serve as a suggestive foil for other messengers in the play (*e.g.*, the Captain, the First Ambassador, perhaps Gertrude [*viz.* Ophelia's death], perhaps the Ghost)?

As always, how, when, and toward what end?

Voltimand, member of the Danish court *(See **Cornelius and Voltimand**)*

Reading: Suggestions

Read each scene three times.

The first time, read however best suits you to get the characters, plot, and the overall shape of the scene. Reading aloud is especially helpful.

The second time, read more slowly, making notes of places in the text you'd like to highlight for closer analysis for any reason, from what the words mean to why the character is taking that rhetorical tack to larger issues the passage touches on.

The third time, read the scene aloud or follow along with a recorded performance. Dimming the video screen helps deflect the influence of directorial choices regarding costumes, set, action, etc. Just focus on the language.

It may prove useful to set up the following initially and update them as you progress through the play:

1. A spreadsheet of who is in which scene. Who are these people? How frequently are they on stage? To whom does each scene "belong"? Larger patterns can emerge from collecting this information and then looking back at it later.

2. A character page for each major character (in *Hamlet,* you'll need at least the following: Hamlet, Horatio, Claudius, Gertrude, Polonius, Laertes, Ophelia. You might want a page for the minor characters as well; Cornelius/Voltimand, Rosencrantz/Guildenstern, Fortinbras, Clowns, etc.) Write a

sentence or two summarizing each character's every appearance in the play.

Act 1

Study Guide and Questions:
Act I.i-ii

Because Act I sets up everything that follows, the guide for this act is presented in two parts (I.i-ii and I.iii-v) to encourage greater focus and depth.

Before beginning work on I.i-ii, readers are encouraged to familiarize themselves with "A General Introduction to *Hamlet*" (*pp. 47-50*) and with the "Character" entries on Bernardo, Francisco, the Ghost, Marcellus, and Horatio.

A note on Horatio: Horatio is a friend of Hamlet's from the University of Wittenberg, a university that carries as much symbolic weight as M.I.T. or Juilliard or any school known for excellence in specific fields. In Wittenberg's case, it's theology (a.k.a., philosophy).

Horatio is extremely intelligent, so much so that he baffles the guards every time he opens his mouth—this can have a strong comedic effect, especially in the opening scene; if you have trouble understanding what he's saying, it's because you're supposed to have trouble. The guards certainly do; the groundlings probably did as well.

Study Guide and Questions, I.i

1. The play opens at the changing of the guard at Elsinore castle. Who is on watch (standing guard) when the play begins? Who is coming on duty? Who is the first to speak?

Shouldn't that line belong to the other guard? What atmosphere does Shakespeare set up right away with how backwards that is?

2. The opening lines of the play are either in prose or display caesurae in almost every line. Which? What's the line that answers that question?

3. Give the dramatic reasons behind your answer to Question #2. Why would Shakespeare want that here? What's happening?

4. List the professions of all characters on stage at line I.i.27. One of these is not like the others; why is that character there? Provide the lines that answer that question.

5. Restate the following lines in contemporary, nuanced language:

> What are thou that usurps't this time of night,
> Together with that fair and warlike form
> In which the majesty of buried Denmark
> Did sometimes march?
>
> (I.i.50-53)

6. Horatio's lines "Before my God, I might not this believe/ Without the sensible and true avouch/ Of mine own eyes" (I.i.60-62) contain a Shakespearean version of a bit of everyday wisdom. What is it?

7. Restate the following lines in contemporary, nuanced language:

> In what particular thought to work I know not,
> But in the gross and scope of mine opinion
> This bodes some strange eruption to our state.
>
> (I.i.71-73)

8. In the next speech, Marcellus wants to know something. What (language question)? Why, very specifically (character question)?

9. Describe the character of "young Fortinbras"—what's he like?

The next questions concern lines 116-129.

10. Restate I.i.116 in contemporary, nuanced language.

11. Define: "graves stood tenantless"

12. Define: "the sheeted dead"

13. Define "gibber"

14. Define "stars with trains of fire"

15. Define "disasters in the sun"

16. Lines 125-129 basically consist of Horatio saying "Yep; I was right." How so, and to which earlier line does this refer? What possible character flaw is hereby revealed? *(Note: Foil Relationship Alert: Remember this moment as the play proceeds.)*

17. Line 131 has a feminine ending. Locate one or two weaknesses lurking within this line or this character or this situation or all three.

18. Line 133 ends in a caesura. What happens in that silence (and again at 136 and 139)?

19. At line 144, Horatio says "Stop it, Marcellus!" Marcellus's response, "Shall I strike at it with my partisan?" was sure to

get a good laugh from the groundlings. Why? And at whose expense?

20. Marcellus's line "Shall I strike at it with my partisan?" (I.i.144) is one of those almost throw-away lines that contains the entire crux of a play's problem. If you've read *Hamlet* before, explain how this works.

21. The guards go after the Ghost with their spears. If the actors have played the preceding bits of the scene properly, this is a great and necessary moment for tension release. Pick three places earlier in the scene that the actors need to imbue with *extreme* tension and fear that will find its release here. Why did you choose these three in particular to build to this moment?

22. What makes the Ghost disappear? There's a particular (and very traditional) binary image being set up here that has to do with good/bad—which? (*Note: Keep track of this throughout the play; it'll return.*)

23. Horatio describes some event as "The morn in russet mantle clad/Walks o'er the dew" (I.i.172-73)—what does that mean?

24. At the end of the scene, Horatio proposes a course of action. What is it?

25. Render I.i.177 in contemporary, nuanced language.

26. Just as I.i begins strangely, it also ends strangely. What technical feature is missing?

27. Keep your eye out in I.ii for that missing feature—it's going to show up in a very strange place. When you find it, come back to this question and provide the actual lines (formal

citation). *(Note: Shakespeare's regulars would be waiting for it and surprised and unsettled by its absence; it's like when music prepares you for an ending, but then one doesn't happen. Nifty little bit of audience psych-out, that; it lends triple emphasis when it does finally show up.)*

Study Guide and Questions, I.ii

1. Judging from the technical features of Claudius's first speech, what are your initial impressions of his intelligence and his relationship to his court?

2. Poor Cornelius and Voltimand have to share their single line in this scene: "In that, and in all things, we will show our duty" (I.ii.40) There's duty again. Doesn't seem like Claudius is asking all that much—go deliver a message. But when you remember the saying "Don't kill the messenger," things get a little bit darker. Claudius is actually going to get one of two answers: a letter or Cornelius's and Voltimand's heads. If he gets a letter, what does that mean? And if he gets their heads?

Note: This is the propositional logic methodology that has everything to do with Wittenberg (see Introduction, pp. 7-12). We're going to see Hamlet using this same information discovery method very soon.

Foil Relationship Alert: Hamlet/Claudius. Yes, really. Seems counter-intuitive, doesn't it? Yet their approach to ways of knowing is remarkably similar.

3. Claudius begins by mentioning that his brother's death is "green"—meaning what?

4. He continues by pointing out that "so far hath discretion fought with nature." First of all, "so far" here has nothing to do with time (contemporary usage: "Up until now"); he means something else entirely. Restate his line in contemporary, nuanced language.

5. Continuing with "discretion fought with nature"—okay, we have a binary in conflict here. With a little bit of intellectual creativity, this one will map onto love and duty (of course).

Which term (discretion/nature) maps onto which term (love/duty)? Explain.

See again: Foil Relationship. They're everywhere. Can't turn around without tripping over them in this play.

6. Claudius resolves that "discretion/nature" problem by saying, basically, that human beings can do two things at once. What two things specifically? (Focus particularly on I.ii.6-7.)

Note: Claudius introduces Gertrude as, "our sometime sister, now our queen" (I.ii.8). Herein lies the incest problem: Although she and Claudius share absolutely no blood, she legally became his sister when she married his brother. This marriage is incestuous legally, not biologically.

7. Claudius's first 16 lines generally concern one thing. What? *(Hint: What is he thanking his court for?)*

8. The rest of his speech concerns the situation with Norway and ends with the word "duty" (which is echoed by Cornelius and Voltimand). So the speech not only moves from death to death but love to duty. If you were going to call this foreshadowing, you'd be right. How will this play out in Claudius's plot and character arc? (If you've read the play before, answer how it does play out; if you've never read the play before, make a prediction as to how it should play out, based on this.)

9. Claudius next turns to Laertes, who, like Hamlet, was also called home from college for the funeral. Laertes asks him for something. What is it?

10. And what is Claudius's response?

11. Backing up to line 47 for a moment: "The head is not more native to the heart"—head/heart alert (duty/love). Pay attention to words like that. Hand/mouth is also offered here (what you do [hand] versus what you say [mouth]). Claudius is basically trying to unify all of these usually opposing binaries here (and elsewhere) as though there's no tension. How does this echo what he does in his first speech?

12. Literally (still with the same lines discussed in the previous question), Claudius is claiming close kinship with Laertes's father (Polonius), equating Polonius's motives and actions with those of the throne. *(Foil Alert: Claudius/Polonius.)* For which characters and other entities does Claudius see himself serving as a father figure?

13. Okay, so now that Laertes is dealt with (for now), we finally (finally!) get to meet our title character. Explain exactly what he means by his first line I.65 (the footnote will help you out). Bevington notes that this line is usually played as an aside, but it need not be. What is the effect on the audience's first impression of Hamlet if it is played as an aside? And if it isn't?

14. Now for some fun with Gertrude. Check out the first verbal moods she uses: "Cast," "let," "Do not... seek". All imperatives. (Such a mom. Do this; don't do that.) She could be ordering him or she could be imploring him. Two different things. If it's the first, duty compels him to obey her. If it's the second, love compels his obedience. (There it is again.) But which is it? Can it be both? Are we given any clues here?

15. She continues, "Thou know'st 'tis common," meaning, as the footnote tells us, "everyday, usual." Hamlet picks up on that

word, though, and says, "Ay, madam, it is common." On the surface, he's agreeing with her literal meaning. "Yes, everything dies." However, the word "common," which Bevington notes has a "vulgar" meaning, packs a really, really powerful punch when you consider why he's so upset with her. What is Hamlet calling his mother here?

16. She responds stichomythically. Depending on your take on her character, this stichomythic response can indicate several things. List a few; you can decide which it is later (and if you're playing Gertrude, you're going to have to decide).

Note: Before moving on to Claudius's next speech, you might want to go back and answer the last question for I.i.

17. Claudius's next speech goes from I.ii.87 to 115. Gertrude's next statement takes only two lines. Taking both the content and the length of those two speeches into account, read Hamlet's next line. What do you learn from this? How can you get that to mesh with that whole "common" thing?

18. Claudius basically says "Excellent; Hamlet's such an obedient boy—time to start drinking." He gives the order that every time he drinks, something will happen. What? And what do you make of this practice with regard to his leadership qualities and fitness to rule?

19. Pertaining to Question #18: Explore how the Hamlet/Claudius foil relationship is working at this moment.

20. Enter the first of Hamlet's major soliloquies. Lines 131-132 tell us what he wishes he could do and why he won't. What, and why not?

21. Lines 135-6 introduce the imagery of the garden (pay attention to gardens in this play) and also to the idea of "growing to seed"—what does "growing to seed" mean and why is it bad for a garden to do that?

22. How much time elapsed between the funeral and the wedding?

23. Restate the lines about how Hamlet, Sr., treated Gertrude in contemporary, nuanced language.

24. Restate the lines about how Gertrude felt about Hamlet, Sr., before his death in contemporary, nuanced language.

25. Explain "incestuous sheets."

26. Based on the language of this soliloquy: In Hamlet's opinion, has Gertrude betrayed her love or her duty? Which lines are your evidence?

27. Last line: "But break, my heart, for I must hold my tongue" (I.ii.159). Love and duty are in there; identify the specific words that indicate "love" and "duty." (The love/duty duality is everywhere.)

28. Before Hamlet can wallow or get angry or soliloquize his intensely awful feelings any more, Horatio, Marcellus, and Bernardo come in. Hamlet's surprised to see Horatio and asks him why he's not still at school. Horatio responds "A truant disposition"—what does that mean?

29. "Truant disposition" is actually a lie, and it's a very kind thing for Horatio to say there. How?

30. What does "followed hard upon" mean in line 179?

31. "Thrift, thrift, Horatio!" Explain lines 180-181 both literally and figuratively. (This verges on the disgusting; forgive me for asking you to think this way, but it's not only the "rotting food" that's—at least in the language—getting "used" twice, here.) (Also: think back to "garden grown to seed." Wasting and rotting have just officially become unmistakably important in this play; we'll see it again later... poor Ophelia... but I anticipate.)

32. Next, Hamlet freaks Horatio out completely. How?

33. Horatio and Hamlet's lines from 193-223 involve frequent stichomythia. Why? How is Hamlet feeling here?

34. What is Hamlet doing in the caesura in line 224?

35. Why do "All" respond stichomythically at line 226? (Anything to do with love or duty? Remember to consider individual characters separately.)

36. Next we have a scene that feels almost like a courtroom, in which Hamlet "examines" the star witness, Horatio. You could argue that this bit's in prose—how could you justify that, especially given the presence of the guards (whom Hamlet outranks by light-years)? You could also argue that this bit is in poetry—Horatio's line at 242 certainly is (with a feminine ending, even if you poetically contract "mod'rate") —and rife with caesurae. How could you justify all those caesurae? Finally, which (poetry or prose) would you, as a director, choose here, and why?

37. Horatio says the Ghost didn't stick around for very long; Bernardo and Marcellus contradict him. We have three witnesses here for one event giving conflicting evidence. Horatio gets the last word. What's the effect of Horatio

getting the last word? *(Hint: What does everyone on stage do next? Including "nothing"?)*

38. Hamlet next pulls out a lawyer's trick—"His beard was grizzled—no?" Grizzled—no footnote for that; what does it mean? Horatio's answer reveals the lawyer's trick (he says "A sabled silver"; is that a synonym for "Grizzled" or not?) and establishes his own credibility as witness. How? How should this exchange be played?

39. The big question Hamlet is asking right about now is what? It's going to be the question that drives the first half of this play.

40. Shakespeare establishes "eye-witness testimony" as being a very compelling form of evidence from lines 222 to the end of the scene, from Horatio's "swearing" ("As I do live") that it's true to Hamlet's decision to go see for himself, ending with the couplet: "Foul deeds will rise/ Though all the earth o'erwhelm them, to men's eyes." (Even the word "overwhelm" has to do with whether or not something is visible.) Find every word you can that has to do with seeing, truth, hiding, etc., in this last section (I.ii.222-263).

Study Guide and Questions: Act I.iii-v

Act I, Scene iii Overview:

In this scene, we're introduced to a family of Danish courtiers: Polonius and his children, Laertes and Ophelia. (We've met Laertes briefly; we know he has permission to go back to college in Paris.)

Polonius: Polonius is a courtier. This means he is of "gentle" (upper-class) birth but—in his case—he is *not* nobility. (He has no title—he's not an earl, or a baron, or a duke.) His central ambition is to be as close as possible to the seat of power in Denmark. Right now, that's King Claudius; in the future, that will be Claudius's heir, Prince Hamlet. How Polonius achieves that closeness is up to him; in this scene we see him laying the groundwork for future plans. Watch his interaction with his daughter and his advice to his son very closely; in the future, watch how he interacts with Claudius. Polonius's power is of very limited scope—it all depends on others; he will manipulate everyone around him (or try) to place himself to advantage.

Laertes: We know he wants to go back to college in Paris. We know he's not nearly as intelligent or scholarly as Hamlet and Horatio. He's upper class but has no title. Pay close attention to how he responds to his father's commands for obedience, and also pay close attention to his relationship with his sister. Laertes really isn't a bad guy at all—he seems a reasonably obedient son and a relaxed, open enough brother that his sister feels comfortable teasing him. Laertes and Ophelia seem to have the only healthy family relationship in the entire play.

Ophelia: Ophelia is a good, obedient daughter, everything she's supposed to be as a young lady of gentle birth (but again, not nobility—just upper class) of her time. She has a bit of a backbone— we can see this in how she teases her brother—but her options for her future are few: she can make an advantageous marriage (which is what her father, Polonius, wants) or she can enter a convent. That's pretty much it. Prince Hamlet, we learn, is romantically interested in her. There are social barriers to their relationship, though, and Polonius will point these out: Hamlet is a Prince and will (probably) have to marry to the political advantage of Denmark and not where his heart leads him. Ophelia's family just isn't politically powerful enough to make her an attractive candidate for such a marriage.

Study Guide and Questions, I.iii

1. Line 4: Explain the stichomythia.

2. In lines 5-9, Laertes gives Ophelia some advice. What is it?

3. Beginning with line 29, Laertes warns Ophelia of the dangers involved in pursuing a relationship with Hamlet. What is the primary danger?

4. At line 39, Laertes mentions a "canker"—this is in keeping with the imagery of rotting and wasting that will occur throughout the play. Explain how "The canker galls the infants of the spring" involves rotting and wasting.

5. Still on line 39: In combination with earlier images of rotting and wasting, this line in its larger context equates Ophelia with "food"—something that can be consumed or something that can be left to rot. Connect this to your response to Question #3 and explain the connection.

6. Ophelia's response to Laertes's advice and warning occurs in lines 45-46. Does she agree to follow it?

7. At line 47, Ophelia comes in with an imperative verb: "Do not…." (Interesting who in the play uses imperative verbs— pay attention to this; a larger pattern might emerge.) Although she is female and thus socially in a "weaker" position, she gives Laertes (the more socially powerful male) her own bit of advice in what follows. What is it?

8. Polonius shows up and tells Laertes to hurry up, he's going to miss his ship. Then he spends the next 23 lines talking. Explain what this says about his character.

9. Restate all of Polonius's advice to Laertes in contemporary, nuanced language, beginning with "Give thy thoughts no tongue."

10. Compare the number of lines each piece of advice requires. Which pieces of advice get the longest expression? If the wordiness of the advice indicates how much relative importance Polonius assigns to it, which advice does he reveal as the most important? What does that say about what he values?

11. The layout of line 85 is a little bit confusing. Is it stichomythia? Or caesura? Consider what it would mean either way, and then decide which it is, explaining why you've decided for either stichomythia or caesura and why you've decided against the other.

12. After Laertes finally leaves (remember, he was already late when the scene started), Polonius turns his attention to Ophelia. Her obedience as a daughter is evident in their first exchange (lines 89-90). How so?

Interlude

The next exchange implies something that would have been beyond obvious to Shakespeare's audience but can be opaque to 21st-century readers. The scene between Polonius and Ophelia involves both an interrogative section ("Tell me the truth, daughter. What's up with you and Hamlet, and what's your evidence?") and a decision (Polonius embarks on a plot which he has to hide from everyone, especially Ophelia.)

It works out, like everything else in this part of the play, as a "Given/If-Then/Therefore" propositional logic problem.

Polonius's goal is to get Ophelia married to Hamlet. Because she is not from a politically powerful family, there is only one way to guarantee that marriage: if Hamlet compromises her reputation and her honor beyond repair. (Basically, if they sleep together—although it need not go quite that far.) What you might call a "shotgun wedding."

Nice father, hm?

So here's how his logic works:

Polonius's Big Question: Is Hamlet in love with my daughter?

Polonius's Method (Propositional Logic Style) for Finding the Answer:

GIVEN Ophelia's information, which seems to indicate Hamlet loves her,

IF I forbid her to spend time with him, and

IF he really is in love with her,

THEN Hamlet will double his efforts to get close to her.

IF that happens, and nature takes its course (as it often does with people in love),

THEN her honor will be compromised and

THEREFORE they will have to marry.

IF Hamlet is not in love with my daughter, and

IF I forbid her to spend time with him

THEN he will leave her alone, and

THEREFORE her reputation won't suffer, and she can marry someone else.

It's sort of the perfect plan—Polonius can, by doing the wise and right thing for a father to do, find out how far Hamlet's affection goes. Either result works fine for him, but it's actually better for him if Hamlet and Ophelia sneak off somewhere and get physical, because they will have to marry, and then he gets to be the next King's father-in-law and quite likely the King-after-that's grandfather. You can't be closer to the throne than being related to it. Worst-case scenario? There's no love there, and Ophelia remains on the marriage market with her reputation intact.

So that's what Polonius is figuring out and embarking on in the remainder of his scene with Ophelia.

The crucial things here are:

A. His "If/Then" methodology (Propositional Logic)—it's a foil for other, larger situations in the play (specifically, Hamlet's, 'though that doesn't get set up 'til the end of Act I).

B. His secrecy—he can't tell anyone what he's doing (again, a foil for Hamlet's situation in the play, and Claudius's, as well).

C. His "spying"—he will manipulate people into revealing the truth without seeming to do so (again, a foil for Hamlet's plan to spy from behind the concealment of feigned madness).

D. His willingness to sacrifice honor (his daughter's; his family's) to achieve his desired ends (political power). Here he's a foil for Claudius.

E. The fact that his plan depends in some way on someone's love/lust for a woman (again, look at what Claudius did and part of his motivation).

End Interlude

13. In light of the interlude section, above, please restate lines 127-136 as something a contemporary father might say to his teen-aged daughter.

14. Explain how Ophelia's last line in this scene echoes not only the language but in some ways the larger stakes of Cornelius's and Voltimand's earlier response to Claudius.

15. Finally, explain very briefly how the "love/duty" dilemma that's an element of everything in this play has been set up for Ophelia—where does her love lie, where does her duty lie? It's not entirely a "neat" problem here; she's a person, yes, but she's also a pawn. You can explain it from her point of view or Polonius's; your choice—just label your response accordingly.

Act I, Scene iv Overview:

This is mostly a logistical scene, although it does contain elements that resonate with what's come before and foreshadow what's coming after in some interesting ways.

The scene starts with Horatio asking Hamlet what's up with the cannons. Hamlet responds at some length. From this we learn that Horatio is not native to Denmark, which places him entirely outside any investment in what happens at court except in two ways:

A. Very generally: As a citizen of this world, he would hope that all people behave rightly and justly and judge all things fairly and in accordance with good principles.

B. Very specifically: Hamlet is his best friend.

Study Guide and Questions, I.iv

1. Restate lines 14-17 in contemporary, nuanced language.

2. Lines 24-36 are one sentence. We get a lot of end-stopping here. End-stopping can indicate a character of lesser intelligence, but it can also indicate a very intelligent character who is off his game for some reason. The fact that Hamlet is a student at Wittenberg indicates that he is very, very intelligent; why in this particular moment in the play might he be so off his game? Acting less than perfectly smoothly? *(Note: The generalities are obvious [his father's dead, Claudius married his mother]; think very specifically about where and when this scene takes place and then answer accordingly.)*

3. Restate lines 24-36 as a much simpler statement, beginning with "Sometimes some men, no matter how good they are otherwise, ..."

4. At line 35, Hamlet's use of the word "corruption" connects to the imagery of rot, disease, and waste. Look up the various definitions of "corruption" (your best source for this is the *Oxford English Dictionary*; it's online) and provide them here.

5. The Ghost shows up. Hamlet's response is in lines 39-56. Please restate lines 40-44 (ending with "speak to thee") in contemporary, nuanced language.

6. Those same lines contain the question Hamlet will have to answer in the first half of the play. What is it?

7. Horatio's line 58 is an example of what dramatic device?

8. Lines 60-64 contain several instances of stichomythia. Although this moment requires a decision, there's not a caesura in sight. Explain why stichomythia is used here.

9. Hamlet's lines 66-7 contain another element of Hamlet's really big question. How so?

10. The dangers these characters note that the Ghost might pose to Hamlet are: to his life, to his soul, and to his mental stability. Which character worries for Hamlet's sanity, and how is that consistent with that particular character? In which lines? What might the Ghost do that might drive Hamlet insane?

Interlude

This is our first real indication of the question of insanity in this play, so it's crucial to note what things these characters believe cause insanity. This particular moment foreshadows something that will happen with Hamlet and Ophelia, individually and collectively, later in the play, so pay attention now.

End Interlude

11. What does Horatio mean by "Be ruled" (I.iv.80)? Connect this to love and duty somehow.

12. "By heaven, I'll make a ghost of him that lets me!" (I.iv.85). What does this line say about Hamlet's character?

13. Hamlet orders Marcellus and Horatio "away." Explain how it is their duty to obey him and their duty not to.

14. "Something is rotten in the state of Denmark" (I.iv.90). Marcellus's incredibly famous line deserves a moment of attention. Prior to now we've been presented with questions of rotting as a danger, as a process, as something to be avoided. But Marcellus's simple declarative ("is rotten") makes the issue more immediate. It's not what's coming; it's already here. He does not mean the Ghost, though. The Ghost is a symptom of something larger. What that "something" might be is indefinite (especially to Marcellus, who's not high rank, not powerful, and not terribly deep or profound—even though he does seem to get some of the best lines). The fact that it's indefinite connects to Hamlet's larger question. But let's end with a fun question in this scene.

Explore various possible reasons why Marcellus, of all characters, gets these great lines (*e.g.*, "Shall I strike at it with my partisan?" [I.i.144]; "Something is rotten in the state of Denmark" [I.iv.90]). Remember Shakespeare's audience in all its socioeconomic variety; Marcellus's lines have to work for everyone.

Study Guide and Questions, I.v

1. The Ghost claims to be Hamlet's father, and claims that Claudius murdered him. How, very specifically, did Claudius commit that murder? Provide the actual lines (formally cited) and then see if you can figure out what the "porches" are in that context.

2. The Ghost lists three things that he lost in that moment of death. What are they, in order? (Provide the specific line and its formal citation.) In persuasive rhetoric, if you're providing a list of three, you put the most important one last. ("Today I bought a mousetrap, a cell phone charger, and a plane ticket to England." It builds to the biggest.) By this standard Western rhetorical practice, what does the Ghost most value in his list of three?

3. The Ghost orders Hamlet to do two things. Not one (that's obvious); two. What are they? (Identify them and provide the specific lines and their formal citations.)

4. Referring still to Question #3, the Ghost sets Hamlet an absolutely impossible task. Explain how his task is impossible—succinctly but thoroughly.

5. Now that you know how King Hamlet was murdered, let's back up for a second—explain the line "So the whole ear of Denmark/ Is by a forgèd process of my death/ rankly abused" both literally and metaphorically. (You'll need to consider a couple of different definitions of "ear" and "Denmark" here.)

6. Lines 114-126: Caesurae or prose? Justify.

7. Hamlet asks Horatio and Marcellus to "be secret." This picks up the thread established by Polonius in I.iii (the Polonius

subplot) in the larger plot (the Hamlet main plot). Hamlet is so insistent on this point that he and the Ghost make them repeat their promises several times between now and the end of the scene. List all the lines where secrecy is mentioned and insisted on (include formal citations).

8. At line 139, Horatio calls Hamlet's lines "wild and whirling" (as well they might be; poor Hamlet's not having a great night, here). Hamlet apologizes that they "offend" him. Horatio replies that he's not offended ("There's no offense"). Hamlet says "Yes, by Saint Patrick, but there is." In that line, Hamlet's referring to a very different offense. What is it?

9. At the conclusion of the whole "Swear" thing, Horatio and Marcellus have to swear "by his sword." Their initial promise is given in 128; what do they swear by in 128? Okay. Now imagine what a sword looks like. How does the shape of the sword incorporate their oath in line 128 in addition to making their promise a personal one to their best friend/prince? Now explain how this works in terms of love and duty. (It may be one, or both, and it may work differently for Horatio than it does for Marcellus.)

10. Finally, Hamlet sets up how he may endeavor to draw a cloak of secrecy (inky cloak, much?) around what he has to do next. "As I perchance hereafter shall think meet/ To put an antic disposition on –" (180-181). This is at least in part a very specific reassurance to Horatio, pertaining to Horatio's earlier worry. How so? (If you've read the play before, you know how this plays out. If you haven't, you'll soon see.)

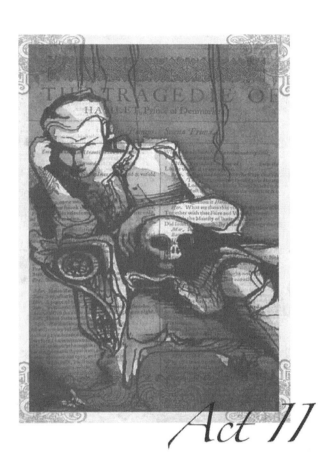

Act II

Study Guide and Questions: Act II

There are several important words in this act that don't have footnotes. Notes on these are interspersed throughout this section.

Overview:

Remember that Shakespeare's Acts II generally do two things: They deepen the main plot and introduce or expand on the sub-plots.

At the end of Act I, the main plot involves Hamlet and the Ghost's directives (Is the Ghost his father's spirit? Or a creature from Hell sent to tempt him into murder, thus damning his immortal soul? In other words, did Claudius murder Hamlet, Sr.?); the sub-plot belongs to Polonius (*i.e.*, "Is Hamlet in love with my daughter, Ophelia? And, if so, how to work that to my and my family's advantage?") There's also the small matter of Fortinbras, Jr., and his invading army.

A new question (part of the main plot) was introduced at the end of Act I: How Hamlet will figure out the question of Claudius's alleged guilt. He's already warned Horatio that he might act insane in order to throw Claudius off-balance and perhaps shake some information loose.

Act II introduces the question of concealment (literally and figuratively) and the various things people hide behind in order to spy out information: Polonius will send Reynaldo to Paris to spy on Laertes (checking up on his behavior at college; following up on all the advice Polonius gave him when he left); Claudius and Gertrude will try to use Hamlet's college friends Rosencrantz and Guildenstern to figure out what's "wrong" with Hamlet; Hamlet will use a mask of insanity to try to destabilize Claudius; as such, Hamlet will use everyone to send misinformation back to Claudius (including

Polonius, Rosencrantz, and Guildenstern). The "spying from a place of concealment" trope (another word for "repeated pattern") will continue throughout much of the rest of the play.

Other tropes appear simultaneously: the question of "What makes a good father?" will shed light on "What makes a good leader or king?" (pay attention to any similarities you can spot between Polonius's and Claudius's decisions and behaviors); the question of sacrifice and self-sacrifice starts to emerge here (in several ways—every time Polonius sacrifices honor or virtue or honesty toward a supposedly "more important" end, pay attention, because Hamlet, too, is making similar sacrifices). Do the ends justify the means? It's tempting to judge Polonius harshly (he's willing to sacrifice his daughter's honor and his son's trust to better the position of his family/himself) but to judge Hamlet sympathetically (he's also willing to sacrifice things he values in order to better the position of *his* family and country, although it's not as obvious), yet their methods are very similar. So, again, do the ends justify the means? Or do context and situation impact how we judge otherwise identical acts? These are huge questions to consider—Shakespeare's really not flinching here.

One way to start to sort all this out is to remember at all times the love versus duty dilemma. In each interaction, ask yourself how each character is (temporarily) resolving the love/duty question, because each character is. It's easy to spot with characters like Rosencrantz and Guildenstern; they love their friend Hamlet, but they must obey their King—they really have no choice (to disobey the king = treason = punishable by death). So they have to choose duty over love unless they want to be martyrs. Polonius, though, as a more fully-fleshed-out character, presents more ambiguity: Is spying on his son an act of love? An act of duty? Valuing love over duty? Valuing duty over love? And duty to what, and love for what? You can think about this one for a long time.

Which perhaps explains one of the reasons this play is considered one of Shakespeare's best.

If you're keeping a spreadsheet of who's on stage when and where they fall on the love/duty question in any given moment, it will really help you understand (and remember) the play.

Push your thinking and explore possibilities—this is a study *guide*; not every question has a right/wrong answer. Some do. Such is the nature of study.

Study Guide and Questions, II.i

1. The edition we're using defines Reynaldo using two phrases. Find them both (they are not in the dialogue but in the textual materials provided by the editor) and supply them here, verbatim.

2. Polonius sends Reynaldo to Paris with money and letters from home—two things any college student might value. What a nice father! But of course, being Polonius, he has to go and complicate things in ways that are less generous and more invasive of Laertes's privacy. He tells Reynaldo to snoop around before actually contacting Laertes, going so far as to tell him what to say to suss out information. In lines 18-36, he presents Reynaldo with a very, very difficult task indeed (sort of a mild echo of the impossible tasks the Ghost gave Hamlet). What is this task exactly, and how is Reynaldo supposed to keep from tarnishing Laertes's reputation as he fulfills it? (Provide the exact line numbers for the lines that support both parts of your answer.)

Note on the word "wherefore" (II.i.38): It means "why." So when Juliet famously asks, "Oh, Romeo, Romeo, wherefore art thou Romeo?" (II.ii.33), she means "Why are you Romeo [Montague]?" not "Where are you?"

3. When Polonius says, "You laying these slight sullies on my son,/ As 'twere a thing a little soild wi'th'working" (II.i.42-43), what does he mean by "slight sullies"? (You can figure this out from context.) How does this echo his plans for Ophelia *(see I.iii)?* (At least Polonius is consistent.)

Note on the word "'a" (II.i.52): It means "he."

4. Polonius's line "Your bait of falsehood takes this carp of truth" (II.i.64)—what a lovely fishing metaphor. List as many situations as you can think of from the entire play in which someone's "bait of falsehood" takes a "carp of truth"—you don't have to explain them, just list them.

Interlude

Shakespeare's tendency to encapsulate huge swaths of the plot in small, almost throw-away lines is something to look out for in every play (remember "Shall I strike at it with my partisan?" [I.i.144]). You can't spot such lines on a first reading, but knowing they're always there can make for much greater confidence reading Shakespeare—you can keep an eye out for them during a second read-through. This is especially useful for classroom teachers who don't always get to choose which play they teach; Shakespeare will help you out if you know—and remember—to let him.

End Interlude

5. Polonius continues (because he does love to prattle on) by saying, "And thus do we of wisdom and of reach,/ With windlasses and with assays of bias,/ By indirections find directions out" (II.i.65-67). "By indirections find directions out" is a great line—very succinct—but let's focus on "we of wisdom and of reach." Responding to Questions #5.a. and #5.b. requires thought and exploration; the "answer" can't be

found in the text. Push your thinking here, and remember everything you know about Polonius and also everything you feel about Polonius. Both are important.

   a.   What does he mean by "wisdom"? How does Polonius define what it means to be wise?

   b.   What does he mean by "reach"? The footnote says "capacity, ability", but push this a bit farther. How does Polonius define "reach"? (Hint: What matters to him?)

Follow-up note on Question #5: You may experience some initial confusion with questions like this; they don't have stable or certain answers. If you can't prove your responses, remember that there is always room for the human in the Humanities.

6.   Next we get Ophelia, who is truly upset. She describes—at length—Hamlet's appearance. Please restate each detail she provides regarding his appearance from lines 80-86 in contemporary, nuanced language. *(Hint: There are six details total.)*

7.   Polonius's response isn't quite what one would expect of a caring father. A contemporary equivalent situation helps illustrate this. A young woman runs to her father because a young man she knows (and sort of likes) from school just burst into her bedroom looking like a complete lunatic…

Teenaged Daughter:	I'm so freaked out!
Caring Dad:	Are you okay?!

But no. That's not Polonius's response. In a way, his response (line 86) reveals his whole plan. How?

A note on the word "mad": It means "insane" (as in "madman") not "angry."

8. From Ophelia's description, Hamlet's wild appearance was matched by what he actually did (seeming/being). For this question, divide her descriptions into moments of action: what Hamlet did first, second, third, &c., ending with his actually leaving, and draw (as well as you can) stick figures illustrating each moment Ophelia describes. (Don't worry if you've no artistic talent to speak of. This will help you visualize the scene—have fun with it.) You're going to need at least four frames to represent each position (If you assign "he lets me go" to its own frame, you'll need five).

9. Polonius is still caught up in his own interpretation of what Hamlet's appearance and actions mean, never mind the absolute breach of courtesy/manners/trust Hamlet displayed by actually entering Ophelia's private chambers. In Shakespeare's day, that would have been as shocking as if Hamlet burst in on her taking a shower today—Very Shocking Indeed. Still missing is any question of or comfort for Ophelia's feelings here. (No "Honey, are you okay?" or "Oh, how scary! Have a hug. You're safe." Nope. None of that.) In Polonius's response (lines 103-109), he says four things, in order.

   a. What is the first thing he says he'll do?

   b. Next, he provides an explanation or interpretation of Hamlet's actions. What is it?

   c. Then he says, "I am sorry." Do you have any idea what he's apologizing for here? If so, what is it?

   d. In line 109, Polonius does something truly awful. What is it? (Remember how upset Ophelia is and how shocking Hamlet's actions really were, given social norms of the time.)

Interlude

When Ophelia says, "I just did what you told me to, Dad," Polonius again states his favorite conclusion. He's stated it three times now. Let's pull back a little bit and remember that at least the first half of this play is all about the methods by which people figure out information:

When Polonius told Ophelia to tell Hamlet she couldn't see him anymore, he was setting up that "If/Then" propositional logic equation. (See the study guide for I.iii if you need a refresher on the specifics.) So here's how it seems to have played out:

IF Hamlet is in love with my daughter, and

IF I forbid her to see him, THEN he will redouble his efforts to see her and compromise her honor, and

THEREFORE they will have to marry—but what's the harm, really, if they're in love?

And this is almost what's happened: Polonius did forbid Ophelia to see Hamlet, and Hamlet did redouble his efforts to see Ophelia, and he really did compromise her honor, although to what extent is open to speculation.

But.

Polonius is taking all of this "appearance"—these "actions that a man might play" (remember the scene with Laertes's clothes? and Hamlet's first lines to Gertrude?)—as proof that Hamlet's totally mad with love for Ophelia. But we in the audience know differently; Hamlet said he might fake an "antic disposition."

End Interlude

10. The following questions refer to Polonius's plan as outlined in the preceding Interlude.

    a. There is a flaw in Polonius's plan. Based on the above interlude, does that flaw lie in the method of propositional logic itself? If yes, how? If no, then the flaw here lies elsewhere—where?

    b. What kind of irony is at play here?

Note: Interestingly, Shakespeare will answer the question of whether or not Hamlet loves Ophelia—and how much—in a later scene, because the audience deserves to have that question answered too. But that won't happen until Act III.

11. In the last speech in II.i, we do get some information of why Polonius is sorry.

    a. Why is he sorry?

    b. This perhaps highlights the difference between "sorry for" and "sorry about"—what is the difference, and how does this scene spotlight that difference?

12. Finally, we get a rhyming couplet (remember pronunciation drift) to end the scene—it's a tangled one, though:

This must be known, which, being kept close, might move
More grief to hide than hate to utter love.

(II.i.120-21)

    a. Take your best shot at untangling it. What does this actually say?

    b. What do you make of the fact that even after delivering the standard Shakespearean "Hey, the scene's ending now" rhyming couplet, Polonius has to speak yet one more syllable? (This says something about his character; explore this one a bit and see what you discover.)

Study Guide and Questions, II.ii

The scene opens with the royal court and two of Hamlet's boyhood friends: Rosencrantz and Guildenstern. These names are truly wondrous and strange. *(See "Introduction," p. 8.)*

1. Claudius opens the scene by saying, "Oh, yes, we've really missed you," and then delivering the truth of why he's called for them. What is that truth?

2. Despite the actual truth of why Claudius sent for Rosencrantz and Guildenstern, his social pleasantry ("We've missed you") might or might not be a lie. It's impossible to tell without greater context. Please briefly list as many things as you can think of in the play up to this point that can have equal but opposite meanings depending on how you choose to read them.

3. Claudius and Gertrude use polite words like "entreat" and "if it will please you"; Rosencrantz points out that their requests carry greater weight. What does he mean by that?

4. Guildenstern then hastens to assure the King and Queen of their compliance. Why does he feel it necessary to do this?

5. How does this initial exchange (lines 1-32) reflect both sides of the love/duty question? Consider all four speaking characters individually.

6. Sometimes the "Thank you" lines are played for comedy—with the King gesturing to Guildenstern when he says "Rosencrantz" and to Rosencrantz as he says "Guildenstern," with the Queen then correcting him as she offers her thanks in the next line. If you were directing the play, would you choose

to play this moment for comedy (*i.e.*, that you can't tell the difference between them—or any of Shakespeare's paired characters, like Cornelius and Voltimand) or would you choose to play it "straight"—that is, that the King isn't confused about (or doesn't care) which is which? Consider the merits of both options as you respond.

7.   When Polonius enters, we expect to hear him say something like "Great news! Our kids are in love!" but instead we get news about Cornelius and Voltimand. Is this Shakespeare faking us out? Or does Polonius need (or imagine he needs) some legitimate business to interrupt the King? (*Note: The text doesn't answer this, but the actors playing the parts and the director directing the play had better have an answer for this question... so again, consider the merits of both possibilities.*)

8.   However you responded to Question #7, Claudius's response touches overtly (and probably inadvertently) on the central issue of Polonius's character (and, via foil relationships and parallel situations, Claudius's vulnerability, Hamlet's problem, and the thing that's going to basically kill everyone before the play ends). How?

9.   Polonius's lines 43-49 present an overt instance of a propositional logic equation: "Unless I've totally lost my mind, I know why Hamlet has lost his." Of course, he is wrong again; he doesn't know that Hamlet is acting. So let's put some pressure on Polonius's logic:

> GIVEN that Hamlet *hasn't* actually lost his mind,
>
> IF Polonius is wrong,
>
> THEN Polonius has lost his mind.

Polonius isn't literally insane, not at all, but figuratively speaking, at least, he is blind. What is blinding him? The first thing is obvious, but try to come up with at least three things. They may be related; still, facets and nuances matter.

10. Again, Polonius surprises the audience. When Claudius says, "Oh, wow, tell me! I've been dying to know!" Polonius says, "Oh, no, no, news of whether or not we're at war with Norway is much more important." Again he lies. How does the audience already know the answer to the war question?

11. We know the answer to Question #10, Claudius knows the answer to #10, Polonius knows the answer to #10. So why does Polonius play this "Make the King wait" game? What's the psychology there?

12. What's the gist of the news from Norway?

13. Finally at line 86, Polonius has the chance to explain Hamlet's madness. Explain Gertrude's response at line 95 in the context of Polonius's preceding speech.

14. Pause to note that great line "brevity is the soul of wit" (II.ii.90). How come Polonius gets all these great sayings, sayings with so much truth in them that they've slipped into everyday circulation, even though he's such a morally grey character? Things like "Neither a borrower nor a lender be," "Brevity is the soul of wit," and "To thine own self be true"—these are famous, inspirational quotations. How is it possible to reconcile these gems of wisdom with their terrible source? (This one will take some thought; explore; see what you can come up with.)

15. Polonius is having so much giddy fun with language (one definition of "art") here:

That he's mad, 'tis true; 'tis true 'tis pity,
And pity 'tis 'tis true

(II.ii.97-8)

Great fun for an actor to play this moment, especially since another then-definition of "art" was "lie"—think "an artful expression" or "the Artful Dodger." So let's slow down Polonius's mile-a-minute brain here. You can answer Questions #15.a.-c. with a single sentence, if you wish.

   a.   Restate: That he's mad, 'tis true

   b.   Restate: 'tis true 'tis pity

   c.   Restate: And pity 'tis 'tis true

16. Suddenly everyone's talking about "faithful" (Polonius at line 115; Claudius at line 130). Why is "faithfulness" suddenly an issue? (Consider the multiple connotations of "faithfulness" as you answer.)

17. In what way is "faithfulness" an issue that's been on the table for the entire play? (Again, consider multiple connotations of "faithfulness.")

18. What foil relationship(s) is/(are) firmly established with this "new" situation? *(Hint: The "new" situation is the Hamlet/Ophelia relationship.)* Which other relationships does that specifically invite us to consider and reconsider? There are at least two, quite possibly more.

19. Polonius is very careful to inform the King and Queen that he had strictly forbidden any relationship between Ophelia and Hamlet. Why?

20. At lines 151-152, the King and Queen exchange their reactions—they're a bit less certain than Polonius, and their lack of certainty prompts him to say lines 153-55.

    a.   What is Polonius really saying?

    b.   Claudius's responses (at lines 151, 155, and 159) are a clear indication of something about his character. He knows he doesn't know something, and he very much needs to. He's got Rosencrantz and Guildenstern trying to find the answer; he asks Gertrude if she thinks Polonius is right; he doesn't immediately take Polonius's word for it nor acclaim him a perfect authority; he asks for other avenues to find further proof. What does this say about his judgment? And what does his judgment say about his ability to rule?

    c.   If Claudius were really innocent of King Hamlet, Sr.'s murder, what are his responsibilities and duties, as King, husband, stepfather, and friend in this situation? How should he seem?

    d.   As he's actually guilty of that murder, what are his additional responsibilities in this situation? Explore this in light of the seeming/being duality suggested in Question #17.c.

21. In response to Claudius's request for other ways to find proof, Polonius has an utterly predictable response. What is it? (Provide the single line from the text.)

22. Claudius's response that they can "try it" indicates that he might not even trust the information of his own eyes. This leads one to pause: Claudius isn't stupid; quite the contrary. Why is it absolutely crucial to Shakespeare that Claudius and Hamlet be fairly evenly matched when it comes to

intelligence? (Granted, Hamlet may be "book smart" and Claudius may be "street smart," but even so...)

Interlude

A reminder about the larger issues in play so far:

1. Love versus duty—how to resolve that dilemma?

2. Ways of knowing ("epistemologies")—propositional logic, spying, confession

3. Kinds of evidence ("proof")—evidence from logic, visual evidence, words as evidence

4. Judgment, wisdom, reason—versus—insanity and other kinds of blindness

5. Seeming versus being—("Seems, madam? Nay, it is. I know not 'seems'" [I.ii.76].)

6. These are all in the service of some even larger questions the play asks us to consider:

   What makes a good person?

   What makes a good leader?

   What makes a good relationship?

   What makes a good parent?

   What is love; what is friendship; what is honor?

   What is a person's primary purpose?

End Interlude

23. The scene between Polonius and Hamlet takes place in prose. Why?

Interlude

Hamlet uses some truly vile imagery as he speaks to Polonius—the juxtaposition of "the sun breeds maggots in a dead dog" and "daughter" and "conception/conceive" gets more awful the more you think on it. Remember the homonymic "sun/son" from Hamlet's initial appearance in the play ("I am too much i'the sun," meaning "Claudius, I'm no son of yours"); also, the sun was used in Shakespeare's time as a symbol of the ruling monarch.

Hamlet uses the word "breeds" and "conception/conceive"; a bit later, when Polonius notes that Hamlet's mad replies are "pregnant" with meaning, it's time to say, "Okay, we've got several references to the same sort of thing, here. Time to back up and pay closer attention."

Here's Hamlet's imagery:

> Sun/son
> Maggots
> Dead Dog

Here's Polonius's grand plan:

Hamlet will compromise Ophelia's honor, and they'll marry, and I'll be the next King's father-in-law.

Here's Shakespeare's imagery (of rot and waste):

Something is rotten in the state of Denmark (I.iv.90).

There is, in fact, method in Hamlet's madness—he knows Polonius's scheme; he's onto it; he thinks it's a spectacularly bad idea and shows Polonius for the truly atrocious father we've thus far seen him to be.

End Interlude

24. Consider the preceding interlude. Hamlet's imagery is exactly parallel to Polonius's scheme: Who is the dead dog? Who is the sun? What are the maggots?

25. Hamlet characterizes Polonius nearly overtly in one section of their scene. Provide the exact lines.

26. Polonius completely misses how badly Hamlet's insulted him (with the truth, really) and proves Hamlet's characterization true when he says "A happiness that often madness hits on" (II.ii.209-10). Explain what the word "happiness" means in that sentence and also how it completely proves Hamlet's earlier insult to Polonius. (This will take some thought. Push your thinking. Remember the context—Polonius was all giddy with happiness earlier and still is—what does it say that Polonius can even use the word "happiness" right now, given Questions #21 and #22?)

27. Rosencrantz and Guildenstern enter as Polonius is leaving. Rosencrantz's line to Polonius, "God save you, sir!" (II.ii.221) is on one level just a polite greeting; on the other, it's deeply ironic (especially if you know the rest of the play). Explain the irony.

28. The scene among Hamlet, Rosencrantz, and Guildenstern is also in prose. Why?

29. Hamlet is pretty sure he knows why Rosencrantz and Guildenstern are there. Provide the line numbers where he states that reason and receives confirmation.

30. Since we already know that Hamlet is incredibly intelligent (not least because he just played a lovely if excruciating game of cat and mouse with Polonius), we're not getting new information here. We do get, however, this:

> EVENT X means that Claudius is thinking and/or feeling THOUGHTS/FEELINGS Y.

Unlike Polonius, who can't set up a fundamentally solid propositional logic equation to save his soul, Hamlet's actually right. What does Hamlet think Claudius is thinking/feeling? "The appearance of Rosencrantz and Guildenstern means that Claudius is thinking and/or feeling _____."

31. Hamlet doesn't need to tell Rosencrantz and Guildenstern that he knows why they're there; he does it to save them awkwardness and discomfort. Why?

32. Rosencrantz tells Hamlet that some players (an acting company) are on their way to Elsinore. Hamlet responds with lines 320-26. Each of his lines (from "He that plays the king shall be welcome") not only refers to the players but also, in some way, to someone in the castle. Locate each of these references within Hamlet's lines and explain whom he's talking about and how it applies. *(Hint: Some foreshadow, some refer to the past, some refer to the present or an ongoing situation. Be flexible in your thinking.)*

Historical note: When Hamlet asks why the Players have left the city and are traveling the country, Rosencrantz says that they're the victims of a new fad for companies made up entirely of child actors (all boys, of course; women were still barred from appearing on stage at whatever age). This is a reference to an actual fad in London and throughout Europe at the time this play was performed—adult companies went out of fashion; it's social commentary from Shakespeare. Bevington provides a specific example of this in his footnote.

33. The section on the boy actors versus adult actors ends with Hamlet drawing a comparison to Claudius in lines 363-68. Explain the comparison in contemporary, nuanced language; bonus points if you can think of a cliché or trite saying that says much the same thing.

Note on lines 367-68: Hamlet's line "if philosophy could find it out" is an overt reference both to propositional logic ("philosophy") and also a clear hint that propositional logic—even set up and applied perfectly— might have inherent limits. An earlier line prefigures this moment: "There are more things in heaven and earth, Horatio,/ Than are dreamt of in your philosophy" (I.v.175-76).

34. Hamlet's line welcoming the Players compares his actions to their own (theirs being, of course, acting). How does this line resonate with the entire play to this point? Explore this.

35. Hamlet's discussion with the Players is also in prose. Why? (Pay close attention to who's on stage here.)

36. Bevington provides ample footnotes for you to sort out that Hamlet's referring to other stories in which sons avenge their slain fathers, so I won't belabor that here—but do take the time to read the footnotes, because otherwise this is all incomprehensible. (The educated among Shakespeare's audience—those in the expensive seats—would know these stories and so could easily follow this part.) Let's look at the language, though, because Hamlet switches suddenly out of prose and into verse. Obviously, he's quoting a play—we even get quotation marks—but it's a play that was never popular and that may only have been performed once. Given that, given everything in this whole scene, explain Polonius's interjection at line 465.

37. As the First Player continues (sort of auditioning for an invitation to perform at court), he's interrupted a few times.

   a. Polonius interrupts him first. Guaranteed this line got a laugh at the Globe. Why?

b. Hamlet interrupts next with the line "The moblèd queen" (Bevington provides a footnote for "moblèd.") Why interrupt here; why echo that phrase?

c. Of course Polonius has to get a word in immediately after Hamlet's—it's terribly repetitive. Why does Polonius speak here (a reference to his character and situation)?

d. Why is Shakespeare forcing us to pay attention to that one phrase?

e. Polonius comes in with a line rubric next, then Hamlet says he'll hear the rest of it later. This means that line 520 ends with a caesura. What happens in that caesura?

38. Hamlet sets up a plot in lines 537-44. What is it?

Interlude

The scene and act end with the second of Hamlet's major soliloquies (the first was "Oh, that this too too sullied flesh..." [I.ii.129-59]). In part, this comes as something of a relief, because this scene has been very, very complicated with so many entrances and exits and clever language and imagery and prose and verse and reminders and resonances that it's sort of nice to heave a sigh of relief and just pay attention to one solo character finally speaking openly, honestly, and truly. It may also be something of a relief for Hamlet; he says, "Now I am alone" (II.ii.549), and he can finally stop acting/performing.

But the relief from that outward show provides no real relief for his feelings (unless you count finally being able to give them voice, but that pales in comparison to what they actually are).

At line 550, Hamlet calls himself a "rogue and peasant slave"—all opposites of a noble, especially of a royal Prince. (If we today wince at the class distinctions, okay, so, we wince; remember that in

Shakesepeare's time, they were taken for granted as part of the world order.)

End Interlude

39. From lines 551-71, Hamlet explains why he, right now, in this moment, feels he is beneath the anonymous itinerant actor—a man without property, birthright, or prospects. What chafes is that he "can say nothing," even with such huge cause. Why?

40. Hamlet continues with a series of questions beginning with "Am I a coward?" and ending with "Who does me this?" (meaning: Who accuses me of cowardice and treats me accordingly?) We've seen no one do that, yet he's acting like someone has. Who has? *(Hint: Think like a psychologist here.)* (It might help you to recall the lines "I have that within which passes show"; they connect really beautifully—explore that for a bit.)

41. Hamlet continues to berate himself for not leaping instantly to vengeance the second the Ghost told him to, referring to Claudius as "this slave's offal"—What is "slave's offal?"

42. Having berated himself for a while, Hamlet then says, "About, my brains!" Bevington's footnote is helpful; thinking of it in military terms might lend it even more power. "About face," the military command this alludes to, is a 180-degree turn. How does "About, my brains!" shift Hamlet's focus from love to duty in the soliloquy? In the larger plot?

43. In the final moments of this soliloquy, Hamlet sets aside his very real emotional/psychological melancholy (And who can blame him? How many relationships has he lost just in the first two acts?) for the necessity of his plan. Find the line where he states exactly how he will know if he has successfully

caught "conscience of the King" (II.ii.605-06)—quote the line (include the formal citation) and then restate it in contemporary, nuanced language.

Act III

Shakespearean Acts III Generally; *Hamlet* Act III in Particular

The "Turn"

Before we embark on the wild ride that is Act III, a reminder about the definition of the "turn" (often, in Shakespeare, the "III.ii turn"), also called the "narrative pivot." This isn't just a structural feature of Shakespeare's plays; it's common to most Anglophone literature written pre-WWII (and much of what comes after, as well).

The definition of the "turn" is this: The moment at which things which were previously only possible become either impossible or inevitable.

In pre-WWII Anglophone literature (broadly defined), this "turn" moment tends to happen half-way through a narrative (no matter what its genre). If you divide the number of pages (or scenes or chapters) by two and turn to the exact middle, chances are excellent that you'll find the turn in the main plot lurking somewhere in the vicinity. If you can figure out which moment is the turn, you can reverse-engineer the major stakes of the overall narrative. Useful when you're struggling to figure out the stakes of a work or are assigned to teach something you've not read before.

The turn in the main plot of *Hamlet* occurs in III.ii in ways I'll point to more specifically throughout this guide; what's especially interesting and fun about *Hamlet* is that every single scene in Act III contains a turn. III.ii contains the main plot turn

(Hamlet/Ghost/Claudius), but each sub-plot gets its own turn as well (Hamlet/Ophelia, in III.i; Hamlet/Theology, in III.iii; and Hamlet/Gertrude, in III.iv).

From Turn to Tragedy

This really is a murder mystery plot, at least to this point; murder mysteries are sometimes called "tragedies with happy endings." The murder mystery is resolved in III.ii, though, so we still have plenty of time to keep this in the realm of tragedy.

One of the fascinating things that emerges from thinking about all of the turns in Act III is the realization that almost every character in this play could stand as the protagonist of his or her own tragedy (if the narrative were re-written)—even Rosencrantz and Guildenstern (Tom Stoppard did that in *Rosencrantz and Guildenstern are Dead*, although you have to squint and get all postmodern about how you define "tragedy").

And the stakes of everyone's tragedy? Love/Duty.

Not every tragic dilemma is a "love/duty" dilemma; that's the big Classical one. *Othello* and *King Lear* are more about "mind/heart"; *Macbeth* is more about "actions/beliefs." (There's plenty more to say about this, but right now it would only be distracting from the main purpose of this guide.)

But Love/Duty is the big one in Tragedy, and everyone in *Hamlet* gets his or her own Love/Duty dilemma.

Except Gertrude. She might, but she might not; there's too much ambiguity in how her role is written to know for sure. The text supports "Bad Gertrude"—a very shallow character or perhaps a very cruel one. She gets no dilemma; she has no conflict between love and duty. The text equally supports "Good Gertrude"—a more complex character who, by III.iv, does confront the love/duty dilemma.

Hamlet is a much more interesting and complex play if we opt for some variation on the "Good Gertrude" reading, but the text does not resolve this ambiguity. Performance must.

Spying

III.i: Claudius and Polonius spy on Hamlet and Ophelia from behind the architecture. Meanwhile, Hamlet spies on Claudius from behind the facade of insanity, using Polonius via Ophelia.

III.ii: Hamlet spies on Claudius from behind the distraction of the play within the play via the Players.

III.iii: Hamlet spies on Claudius from behind the architecture while Claudius's attention is on prayer.

III.iv: Polonius spies on Hamlet from behind a tapestry in Gertrude's chambers. The Ghost appears in such a timely manner that one can assume he has also been spying on Hamlet from beyond.

Horatio (in III.ii) and Gertrude (III.iv) are interesting here; they're only implicated in others' spying activities—everyone else is more actively involved, especially through III.ii. Gertrude's loyalties are a huge question; Horatio's loyalties are sure and never shaken; his love/duty is in alignment pretty much throughout (it wobbles very briefly right at the end). It's interesting to consider them together, for comparison.

With all the spying, if the stakes were lower, Act III could work like a dramatic farce. Spying, mistaken identity—those are features of Roman Comedy. We're still formally right on the line of comedy, but the stakes are so high and the pain so deep that no; still tragedy. Shakespeare: Too clever by half.

Study Guide and Questions: Act III.i-ii

Because of Act III's structural importance, the guide for this act is presented in two parts (III.i-ii and III.iii-iv) to allow for greater depth and focus.

Hamlet's Behavior in III.i

This is one of the more difficult scenes in the play in terms of figuring out the truth behind the words and actions. There's no getting around the fact that Hamlet's treatment of Ophelia is *really* harsh. But perhaps the truth of it is something altogether opposite—as you're reading, remember the phrase "cruel to be kind." Hamlet has a pretty good idea where this all could go—and he's right; his motivation in this scene is to get her out of the castle and away from the ugliness and the danger. Remember Hamlet's line "But break, my heart, for I must hold my tongue"? That applies in his scene with Ophelia. It's a much more interesting scene if what he's doing is killing him on the inside.

In III.i, Hamlet has to make a choice (several, really) between love and duty. Love for Ophelia; duty to his father (if the Ghost was his father; he doesn't know that until III.ii). Love for Ophelia; his duty to Denmark. Love for his father; love for Ophelia. There are probably more; those are the big ones.

And he has to make these choices while seeming to be crazy.

This might be the hardest scene for an actor to play in all of Western Drama. It would be hard enough if all that were going on is what's on the surface—including the English-speaking world's most famous "soliloquy" (scare quotes for a reason; see the questions)—but if what Hamlet's really feeling has to be hidden all the time, how to convince Claudius/Polonius of one thing, Ophelia of something slightly different (which she may or may not miss), while showing the audience that your heart is screaming an objection to all of it... There are reasons why the role of Hamlet is one of the highest aspirations of really good actors. This play is akin to the Olympics of acting.

Insanity: Is Hamlet actually insane? Enough is going on to drive him mad. Still, Shakespeare doesn't answer this question for us; how much can one person—even one with a "noble mind" and a strong will—stand? The best productions put extreme pressure on this issue but don't answer it. One possibility is that his mind is absolutely intact (V.i stands as evidence for this) but that his heart is breaking in every way possible. It's a far more painful play if he doesn't have even the compromised comfort of going insane, and the deeper and more inescapable the pain, the more satisfying the tragedy.

Suicide: Since Hamlet pointed out earlier that "the Everlasting" has "fixed/ His canon 'gainst self-slaughter" (I.ii.131-32), we know Hamlet's not actively considering suicide here. He can no more commit suicide than he can just kill Claudius and be done with it—both risk his immortal soul in ways he's proven unwilling to do. Still, he's been pushed by circumstances to the point where he has plenty to say about it intellectually; his life is much, much harder than he imagines dying might be. Even so, "suicidal" is "an action that a man might play," and as he's fully aware that he's been spied on since at least II.ii, it seems logical for him to assume he's being spied on now—that he has an audience and thus must play a role.

Study Guide and Questions, III.i

1. In the final moments of this soliloquy, Hamlet sets aside his very real emotional/psychological melancholy (And who can blame him? How many relationships has he lost just in the first two acts?) for the necessity of his plan. Find the line where he states exactly how he will know if he has successfully caught "conscience of the King" (II.ii.605-06)— quote the line (include the formal citation) and then restate it in contemporary, nuanced language.

2. Gertrude's next two lines are stichomythic. Why?

3. In their responses to the Queen, Rosencrantz always speaks first, followed by Guildenstern. What is the difference between the kinds of responses they make? *(Hint: Remember they are in a bit of danger here; the King knows they're good friends with Hamlet.)*

4. Now consider the differences between the King's questions to them and the Queen's. They both want to know things, but the kinds of things they want to know are different. What's Claudius's concern? What's Gertrude's?

5. What function does Polonius serve in III.i.25? (Think both in terms of plot and in terms of staging; two slightly different rationales apply here.)

6. Line 25 contains a caesura; Claudius is thinking and deciding. What question is he asking himself, and what's the answer? This all happens silently; you can provide these in blank verse or prose, as you wish.

7. Knowing what's coming in the play-within-the-play scene, explain the irony in III.i.26-27. Also, what kind of irony is this?

8. The caesura in line 31 bears a bit of attention. Claudius commands Gertrude to leave, so he and Polonius can spy on Hamlet and Ophelia. Then he pauses. Then he spells things out for her. The pause involves no thought, no decision, and no action; he knows the plan; he's decided on the plan; Gertrude doesn't leave until a few lines later. What's up with that pause? *(Hint: The pause may belong to Gertrude.)*

9. Restate Polonius's line "We are oft to blame in this [...] that with devotion's visage/ And pious actions we do sugar o'er/ The devil himself." If the line begins "It's often the case that human beings...", how does it end?

10. Define and explain Claudius's reaction to this latest of Polonius's pithy truisms.

11. Hamlet's famous "To be or not to be" speech comes next.

   a. Technically speaking, is this a soliloquy?

Interlude: Claudius

Hamlet is obviously a keen student of drama (remember how he just recited a speech for the Player), and Shakespeare often has fun with the meta level. Hamlet is at least 99% sure he's not alone: Claudius has tried the frontal approach—Rosencrantz and Guildenstern—which failed; his next move was to send for Hamlet personally. (It's Ophelia Hamlet's not expecting to see right now; more on that later). It's logical for Hamlet to conclude he's being watched here.

So the "To be or not to be" speech is supposed to seem to be his innermost thoughts, but in it, he is actually performing what he wants any spies to think he thinks. (Seeming versus being again.)

Never mind who the spies are (Claudius can and has used anyone); it'll get back to Claudius. Claudius is the real audience for what Hamlet's saying in this speech. Claudius is supposed to believe that these are his innermost thoughts.

The "To be or not to be" speech is particularly important as it's the first thing Hamlet has said "to" Claudius since his first two lines in the play: "A little more than kin, and less than kind" and "Not so, my Lord, I am too much in the sun" (I.ii.65 and 67). (If you're keeping a spreadsheet, you'll see that they've not appeared on stage together since that first time—even in II.ii, Claudius exits just before Hamlet enters.) Hamlet has thus had only one brief exchange with Claudius in this entire play so far; the rest of his lines in I.ii were addressed to Gertrude.

We're getting set up for the III.ii turn here. The question driving the first half of the play is WWHD (What Will Hamlet Do)? The question that drives much of the second half is WWCD (What Will Claudius Do)?

End Interlude

b. Why might Hamlet want Claudius to think he's considering suicide?

c. What earlier line of Hamlet's (from another soliloquy) proves he's not? (Give the line in full and the formal citation.)

d. What other (earlier) choice of Hamlet's makes it pretty much certain that Hamlet will in no way risk a mortal sin?

e. In the "To be or not to be" speech, Hamlet doesn't bring up the question of mortal sin; he focuses more on the fear of the unknown as the reason people usually choose to go on living. He instead says, "Thus conscience does make cowards of us all." How is this line aimed at Claudius, in particular? What earlier line from this scene also contains the word "conscience," thus cementing the resonance? (Give the full line and the formal citation.)

f. The answer Hamlet provides to the question "To be or not to be?" can be neatly, if inelegantly, re-stated as "Better the devil you know [life] than the devil you don't know [what happens after death]." So imagine that Hamlet is—while speaking beautiful, painful, quotable poetry—also sauntering across the stage saying, "Oh, Clauuuuuudius... Claaaauuudius... I know you're in heeeeeere.... Better the devil you know, Claudius, than the devil you don't know...."

What are the "devils" Claudius knows? What are the "devils" he doesn't?

12. Consider the earlier line: "Seems? Nay, Madam, it is. I know not seems." We've now been given two opposites for "being": "seeming" (living but pretending) and "not being" (not living). Thanks, Shakespeare—we have a conceptual foil to consider now. How is "seeming" similar to "not being" and how is it different?

Interlude: Ophelia

At the end of the "To be or not to be" speech, Hamlet spots Ophelia, whom he was not expecting to see. "But soft!" is a really, really pretty way to say something that today might come out as "Oh, sh*t!" ('Tis true, 'tis a pity.)

This immediately results in a lightning-fast propositional logic problem; let's work through it with him.

GIVEN that _____ sent for me (and is lurking nearby either in person or by proxy), and

GIVEN that Ophelia is here,

THEREFORE it's a safe bet that _____ reported my actions last time I saw her to _____, who in turn reported them to _____.

(Hamlet [aside]: %#*+!)

GIVEN that Ophelia is a good and obedient daughter who tells her father everything if he asks, and

GIVEN that Polonius is a slimy courtier who will do anything to get into the King's good graces, her appearance right here right now means

THEN she's being used (likely) or she's against me too (unlikely, but can't be ruled out).

(Hamlet [aside]: %#*+!)

IF she's being used (99.999999% probability), and

GIVEN THAT (or perhaps IF) I love her,

THEN I have to get her out of here before things get uglier (but I can't explain why because I'm being spied on and have to appear crazy).

(Hamlet [aside]: %#*+!)

IF she's turned against me (0.000001% probability) and no matter how I feel about her,

THEN no matter how I feel about her, I have to keep her far away from me.

(Hamlet [aside]: %#*+!)

THEREFORE, no matter how I feel (love), no matter how she feels (love), my duty (to her, if she loves me; to Denmark, either way) is to drive her away for her own safety.

(Hamlet [aside]: %#*+!)

THEREFORE I will now switch to prose.

Please note that Hamlet has exactly as much time to figure all this out as it takes him to say this:

"Soft you now,/ The fair Ophelia.—Nymph, in thy orisons/ Be all my sins remembered" (III.i.89-91).

Insane? Thinking that clearly that quickly seems much more method than madness.

End Interlude

13. Okay, given all that logic in the preceding interlude, explain in thorough sentences why Hamlet therefore must switch to prose. What's his objective? What's his plan? When he thought it was just Claudius (or his spies) watching, he was perfectly fine with blank verse; soliloquies are always in blank verse.

On to the specifics of the Hamlet/Ophelia dialogue:

14. Ophelia returns a few gifts Hamlet had given her. He denies having given them to her, and she says he gave them "with words of so sweet breath composed/ As made the things more rich." Restate her lines in contemporary, nuanced language.

15. Let's untangle some Hamlet now. "... the power of beauty will sooner transform honesty from what it is to a bawd than the force of honesty can translate beauty into his likeness." Untangle this, and restate it in clear, contemporary language.

16. Next Hamlet tries to unsettle poor Ophelia. He says, "I loved you once." (Past tense. That has to sting.) Then, "I loved you not." Now what is she supposed to think? He's all over the place here; he's setting something up, though, which comes at the end of his next bit: "Where's your father?" Ophelia's response, "At home, my lord" is utterly, patently a lie. This answers (for Hamlet) one question about how Ophelia will act. Not about what she thinks or feels, how she'll act. What, very specifically, is that question?

17. Reword (phrase by phrase) Hamlet's next line, "Let the doors be shut upon him, that he may play the fool nowhere but in 's own house" in contemporary, nuanced language. What might he mean by "play the fool," in particular?

18. Hamlet keeps saying "Get thee to a nunnery" "to a nunnery" "Go" and "farewell." Find and quote (with formal citations) all of the instances of these phrases in the scene.

19. Why does he say "nunnery" so many times? It might mean "convent" and it might mean "brothel"—answer both ways, and consider how this word may play to Claudius's and Polonius's ears.

20. Regarding the entirety of the Hamlet/Ophelia scene:

    a. This scene can be read as a critique of constraints placed on all women in the Elizabethan era. You could be noble or common (and remember what Hamlet means when he calls Gertrude "common"); you could be a wife/mother, a nun, or a whore. Those were a woman's options; those were how society would view her. There was a singular exception in the person of Queen Elizabeth I, who was never a wife, mother, nun, nor whore, but she was called The Virgin Queen. What evidence can you find in the text that this scene may contain Shakespeare's critique of Elizabethan gender roles?

    b.   Social critique is more often found in Elizabethan comedy than tragedy; what about this non-comedic scene renders it a safe moment for such critique?

21. Ophelia's lament after Hamlet's exit ends with a rhyming couplet. The scene's not over, though. Why might she use a rhyming couplet here?

22. Claudius's speech starts to draw some conclusions. Taking them in order, let's see how he's doing on Professor Hamlet's Wittenberg University: Philosophy 101 midterm:

    a.   "Love? His affections do not that way tend"—Right or wrong?

    b.   "Nor what he spake, though it lacked form* a little,/ Was not like madness"—Right or wrong?

        Note: It was in prose, not blank verse. More meta.

    c.   "There's something in his soul/ O'er which his melancholy sits on brood"—Right or wrong?

    d.   "And I do doubt the hatch and the disclose/ Will be some danger"—Right or wrong?

    e.   Bonus question: Which of the above (a-d) involve irony? How so?

Claudius decides (THEREFORE) to send Hamlet to England, thinking (hoping?) that a change of scene will do him good. He turns to his lab partner, Polonius, and says, "Maybe?"

     f.   True or False: Claudius needs a different lab partner if he wants to pass Professor Hamlet's Philosophy 101 class.

23. In 179-81, Polonius does something very risky. What is it?

24. Consider Polonius's line to Ophelia: Parenting fail? If yes, count (and list) the ways. If not, why not? (This too is a risk, but we don't see how it plays out until much later; it's one Polonius doesn't know he's taking, regardless.)

25. Polonius then compounds with his original risk in lines 184-90. Restate his plan as a list of steps, ending with "And then if all else fails, send him to England."

26. Polonius's plan has a lot of ifs. Propositional logic, or not?

27. Great line for Claudius at the end of the scene: "Madness in great ones must not unwatched go" (III.i.191). He's said he doesn't think Hamlet is mad, though. Why then does he use the word "madness" here, talking to Polonius? (*Hint: He's either using it sincerely or insincerely; the actor playing Claudius must decide which it is.*)

28. Which moment is the turn in the Ophelia/Hamlet subplot in III.i? It's a line or less. Provide it in full with formal citation (or provide the line number at which it happens and explain it). A turn is the work of a moment—a single, brief moment. No more.

29. What moment sets up the turn that's coming in the Hamlet/Polonius subplot in III.iv? Again, a line or less. Provide it in full with formal citation. (If you've not read the play before, return to this question when you've finished reading III.iv.)

Study Guide and Questions, III.ii

1. In this scene, we get the turn and the answer to the big question that's driven the first half of the play: "Is this the ghost of my father, or is it a lying devil sent to imperil my soul?" A single instant answers that question for Hamlet. Provide it in full with formal citation or provide the line number at which it happens and explain it.

2. Complete the following propositional logic statement:

   GIVEN that there is a Ghost who says Claudius murdered my father,

   IF the Ghost is truly my father,

   THEN I must _____.

   IF the Ghost is a devil,

   THEN I must not _____.

   IF Claudius _____,

   THEN I will know the answer.

   GIVEN that Claudius (did / did not) _____,

   THEREFORE I (must / must not) _____.

   Only such a beautifully simple question could provide solid enough framework for all of the complexity woven around it if you want the groundlings to be able to follow it. And they, remember, are the bread and butter of any Elizabethan theater.

Which brings us back to a meta question:

3. Now that you've found the turn, go back to the beginning of the scene and let's see what Hamlet, Professor of Acting 101, has to tell the Player (and what we might learn from this about acting style on the Elizabethan stage).

    Please translate all of the following advice or negative examples into advice for a contemporary group of high school or university actors:

    a. Speak the speech, I pray you, as I pronounced it to you, trippingly on the tongue. But if you mouth it, as many of our players do, I had as lief the town crier spoke my lines.

    b. Nor do not saw the air too much with your hand, thus, but use all gently; for in the very torrent, tempest, and, as I may say, whirlwind of your passion, you must acquire and beget a temperance that may give it smoothness.

    c. Oh, it offends me to the soul to hear a robustious and periwig-pated fellow...

    d. tear a passion to tatters, to very rags...

    e. to split the ears of the groundlings...

    f. who for the most part are capable of nothing but inexplicable dumb shows and noise.

    g. (Given that if the groundlings weren't actually enjoying the play, they'd have left by now. But what just happened? Did Hamlet just insult the groundlings or compliment them?)

> h. I would have such a fellow whipped for o'erdoing Termagant. It out-Herods Herod. Pray you, avoid it.

Got all that? Great. Now Hamlet proves himself his father's son; we'll get back to that in a second. Acting 101 concluded, let's continue with Professor Hamlet's Acting 102 class:

4. Same directions as for Question #3.

> a. Be not too tame, neither...
>
> b. but let your own discretion be your tutor. (Further: How do Hamlet's instructions thus far echo the two-part command given to Hamlet by the Ghost? Different scale, sure, but they resonate. Explore this for a bit.)
>
> c. Suit the action to the word...
>
> d. the word to the action...
>
> e. with this special observance, that you o'erstep not the modesty of nature.
>
> f. For anything so o'erdone is from the purpose of playing...
>
> g. whose end, both at the first and now, was and is...
>
> h. to hold as 'twere the mirror up to nature...
>
> i. to show virtue her feature...
>
> j. scorn her own image... (note: "scorn" is a noun, here)
>
> k. and the very age and body of the time his form and pressure.
>
> l. Now this overdone or come tardy off...

m. though it makes the unskillful laugh, cannot but make the judicious grieve...

n. the censure of which one must in your allowance o'erweigh a whole theater of others.

o. (Skipping ahead a bit) And let those that play your clowns speak no more than is set down for them...

p. for there be of them that will themselves laugh, to set on some quantity of barren spectators to laugh too...

q. though in the meantime some necessary question of the play be then to be considered.

5. Hamlet's basically saying, "Do. This. Right." In his advice, he worries about actors playing to a socio-economically mixed audience, but the Players will perform for the court—a small, upper-class, educated audience. What very specifically is Hamlet worried might happen?

6. We've heard "villain" before:

Hamlet: Oh, villain, villain, smiling damned villain!
        My tables—meet it is I set it down
        That one may smile, and smile, and be a villain.
        At least I am sure it may be so in Denmark.
                      (I.v.107-10)

Hamlet: Bloody, bawdy villain!
        Remorseless, treacherous, lecherous, kindless
        villain! Oh, vengeance!
                      (II.ii.580-82)

Why is the word "villain" thus especially apt at line 43? *(Hint: Re-read the I.v and II.ii soliloquies and then connect both to III.ii.43, explaining how these earlier moments connect and build to this one.)*

7. During the play, Lucianus pours poison into Gonzago's ear. Despite having warned the actors not to interrupt the key moment of the play, Hamlet then starts talking. Why? What's his purpose?

8. Take a look at the two things that prick Claudius's conscience here. What are they?

9. Let's continue to look at this: Claudius can stay seated through the visual re-enactment of one thing but can't stay calm when hearing the words pointing to another. Explain both as though you're explaining to the actor playing Claudius how to act in these moment. Be detailed, and provide his motivations for him.

10. What does Hamlet mean by the line "What, frighted with false fire" (III.ii.264)?

11. Claudius and Polonius both call for lights (Polonius just echoes Claudius, here). Remember that in I.i, dawn made the Ghost disappear; how is the same imagery working here?

12. Why after the court and players leave does Shakespeare give us the brief exchange between Hamlet and Horatio? What purpose does it serve?

13. Finally, Rosencrantz and Guildenstern return and bring Hamlet some information and a message.

    a. What information do they impart about Claudius's mood? About Gertrude's?

    b. What message do they bring and from whom?

   c. Restate this in contemporary, nuanced language: "… you have the voice of the King himself for your succession in Denmark" (III.ii.339-40)?

   d. Why might that not be exactly what Hamlet wants to hear right now? (Think about how succession works on a literal level. What will Hamlet have to do?)

   e. Explain the business with the recorders and how Hamlet uses that image to express his anger at Rosencrantz and Guildenstern.

   f. Why should he be angry with them now, when they're not doing anything worse than they did earlier, for which he forgave them before they even had to say anything?

14. Next, Hamlet is extremely nasty to Polonius. How, exactly? And why?

15. Explain how this particular insult works:

> Hamlet: I will come by and by.
> Polonius: I will say so.
> Hamlet: "By and by" is easily said.
>   (III.ii.383-86)

16. End scene: Hamlet uses a brief moment of alone time to caution himself to one thing, and one thing only. What is it? What command does it echo? Why do we get yet another echo to I.v here?

Study Guide and Questions: Act III.iii-iv

Please review the section on "The Turn" from "Shakespearean Acts III Generally; *Hamlet* Act III in Particular"; the rest of Act III contains two more. Whether we read Ophelia as savvy and speaking in her own kind of protective code in III.i or as too innocent to play that game, the III.i turn comes at the lines "Where's your father?" "At home, my lord"—the first time she lies—or pretends to—in the play. In III.ii, the main plot turns when Claudius leaps to his feet ("The King rises"), thus revealing his guilt. From that point forward, Hamlet knows what his course of action must be—and Claudius knows that Hamlet knows.

In III.iii, we see yet another turn—this in Hamlet's relationship to himself/his soul. In III.iv, we get yet another—in the Hamlet/Gertrude relationship (and also in the important matter of Polonius's own plot, in which his children are implicated).

Study Guide and Questions, III.iii

This is a pretty straightforward scene in terms of plot, character, and action (or inaction)—everything's in motion now—so let's get right to the questions.

1. Summarize the plot of III.iii. You must account for decisions, plans, and next steps that are set up for the following:

a. Claudius's plans for Rosencrantz and Guildenstern (regarding Hamlet).

b. Claudius's and Polonius's plan regarding spying on Hamlet.

c. What Claudius does/doesn't do when he is alone/thinks he's alone.

d. What Hamlet does/doesn't do when he's spying on Claudius.

You can answer Question #1 fully and well with four sentences of plot summary.

2. Line 2 has a feminine ending. What sort of weakness might this indicate? Pay attention to the last word.

3. In Claudius's first speech (III.iii.1-6), lines 1, 4, and 5 are in strict iambic pentameter. If lines in strict iambic pentameter involve some sort of order (real or desired) or establish some "base-line normalcy," then, what sort of order do these lines indicate?

4. Guildenstern's response to Claudius ends, "To keep those many many bodies safe/ That live and feed upon Your Majesty." Line 9 is strict iambic pentameter; locate and identify the "order" herein.

5. Continuing with Guildenstern's line, what does he mean by "feed upon Your Majesty"? This is yet another line referring to ingesting and consuming; connect this line to Hamlet's earlier line, "As the sun breeds maggots in a dead dog."

6. Rosencrantz's response also starts in strict iambic pentameter (if you pronounce "peculiar" as having only

three syllables, which is pretty standard). At which word or phrase does Rosencrantz break iambic pentameter (what is the first substitution)? Give the actual word/phrase. (If you get past line 14, you've gone too far.) Why give this particular word/phrase extra emphasis at this moment in the play?

7. List the lines in the Claudius/Rosencrantz/Guildenstern scene that have feminine endings. Pick one that's not been discussed above, and locate and explore the implied weakness.

8. Rosencrantz gets a couple of great lines: "The cess of majesty/ dies not alone" (III.iii.15-16) and "Never alone/ Did the King sigh, but with a general groan" (III.iii.22-23). Two things here:

   a. Justify Rosencrantz's rhyming couplet. Why's it here? (Think in terms of stagecraft.)

   b. We haven't seen the pithy Marcellus in a while; here Rosencrantz takes over one of his functions—what is it, how, and why now? (Again, think in terms of original performance.)

9. Next we get Polonius. Explain how line 30 is absolutely indicative of his character.

10. Restate "'Tis meet that some more audience than a mother,/ Since nature makes them partial, should o'erhear/ The speech of vantage" (III.iii.31-33) in contemporary, nuanced language. Try to go one phrase at a time; get pretty specific here so you don't lose any nuance.

11. For the first time in the play, we get Claudius alone. Read his soliloquy aloud with an ear for: feminine endings, alliteration, and lines that deviate wildly from iambic pentameter.

    Which lines have feminine endings? Write them out fully, with formal citations.

    a. Consider all of them together. What's the overarching weakness toward which they gesture?

    b. There's a lot of alliteration; what sound is the most dominant to your ear?

    c. Why might that particular sound be the most dominant for this character at this point in the plot?

    d. Which lines are in strict iambic pentameter? Write them out fully, with formal citations.

    e. Considering all of them together, what's the larger order or plot outline (or whatever other interesting pattern you find) toward which they gesture?

12. Look at line 55: This isn't the first time we get a list of three things ending with a reference to Gertrude. Find the other (hint: Ghost) and write it out fully, providing the formal citation, then explain what the line 55 list reveals.

13. Philosophical question for you now: "May one be pardoned and retain th'offense?" That's an important question. Explain how it's important to Claudius, and then explain how it's important to everyone in the audience—and not only in terms of the play.

14. What is the overall gist of Claudius's preparation for prayer (ending with III.iii.72)? What's he worried about?

15. Enter Hamlet. Is his speech a technically a monologue or a soliloquy? How so? How might it also qualify as the one you didn't choose?

16. There are two caesurae in Hamlet's speech. Provide them (write them fully, with formal citations). These are not actions, but actual pauses for thinking. What is Hamlet thinking in both pauses? Write Hamlet's thoughts in the first person.

17. Why does Hamlet decide not to kill Claudius right now?

18. How does that decision echo Old Testament justice ("An eye for an eye")?

19. Of all the so-called deadly sins, the worst is pride—putting oneself before God. Explain how Hamlet has just committed that sin. (*Hint: Think not only in terms of action on the earthly plane but also in terms of the afterlife.*)

20. Now explain the irony of Claudius's closing rhyming couplet.

Study Guide and Questions, III.iv

For III.iv, think visually. Think about staging. Think about who can see whom. And then think about how this scene gives us something we've never seen before, and something Hamlet never thought to see again.

1. In this scene, who can see whom?

    a. Polonius can see:

    b. Gertrude can see:

    c. Hamlet can see:

    d. The Ghost can see:

2. There are two fathers here, and one child. In this scene, the fathers are only visible to the child when dead. How does this suggest (and possibly contain) a larger truth?

3. In the previous scene, Hamlet thinks when he "should" (possibly) act; in this scene, he acts when he "should" (possibly) think. Whiplash—we've been waiting for half of a play for Hamlet to do something; when he finally knows what he should do, he doesn't do it—and then half a moment later, he does something (finally!), but, oh, good heavens, it's the wrong thing. He's been so careful about his judgment for so long that when he finally, finally has the last piece of information he needs—confirmation of Claudius's guilt— something snaps, and his thoughtful, scholarly, noble mind really does get o'erthrown. What snaps? Why? (The answer isn't in the text, but your mind, heart, soul, imagination— wherever you locate such things.)

4. Why does the Ghost show up now? (Consider your answer to Question #12 in III.iii.) What's his purpose? What's Hamlet about to do?

Interlude

So, in two back-to-back scenes, Hamlet (temporarily, at least) doesn't do what the Ghost explicitly told him to do. We've already seen Hamlet delay taking revenge on Claudius; here, the Ghost's command "But taint not thy mind nor let thy soul contrive/ Against thy mother aught" seems also to slip from Hamlet's mind.

End Interlude

---

5. You can argue that Hamlet assumed it was Claudius behind the arras, not Polonius. List as many reasons as you can think of why those assumptions are actually pretty reasonable.

6. How does this scene provide a neat echo of the moment Ophelia reported to Polonius in II.i?

7. Let's think costume/set design for a moment.

> IF we're reading Gertrude properly (as the thing most valued by Hamlet, Sr., Claudius, and Hamlet, Jr.— because the evidence is pretty overwhelming)
>
> AND she's the person Hamlet feels most betrayed by
>
> THEN it is possible that in his rage he is about to lash out at her (BUT he stops himself and redirects that rage and his sword.)
>
> HOW can the costume and set designers visually underscore that with set and costume design?

(Hint: Look up the word "arras" and go from there.)

8. Lines 10-13 contain an example of a particular aural device we've not yet examined in this play.

    a. Which one? (Write out the full definition as well.)

    b. Why might Shakespeare have reserved that aural device until this scene in particular?

    c. What is the difference between "thou" and "you"? *(Note: Research this. The actual answer might surprise you.)* What does this difference reveal about what's happening here?

    d. How are "idle" and "wicked" opposites?

9. Hamlet finally gets his own rhetorical list of three (in III.iv.16-17). Which is the most important? Is it what you'd have suspected?

10. Go back to the moment of the III.ii turn—what's the word that sends Claudius to his feet?

11. This scene gives us much of the information we're going to get regarding how Gertrude is supposed to play V.ii. We have so much to go on, yet so little on which to hang certainty.

    a. List every line, moment, reaction, or reflection-based insight that you could use as evidence to support the position that Gertrude just thinks Hamlet is crazy and that even after this scene she has no clue that Claudius is morally responsible for what is "rotten in Denmark."

b. List every line, moment, reaction, or reflection-based insight that you could use as evidence to support the position that beginning with this scene, Gertrude comes to realize how horribly she's betrayed her son and how vile a creature Claudius really is.

c. Which do you prefer?

d. What staging choices could you make (regarding who's where, where they're looking, how they're standing/sitting/etc.) to support your choice in Question #11.c.?

Act IV

Study Guide and Questions: Act IV

Since we're now past the main turn and all of the subplot turns, from here to the end, things are more straightforward. Ambiguity remains, of course, but as the main plot's possibilities have finally yielded certainty (Hamlet must kill Claudius; Claudius must try to prevent this), Act IV feels much more linear, despite its many surprises.

Structure

Shakespeare's Acts IV usually involve a delay in the movement toward resolution, balanced by the inclusion of some kind of visual spectacle (the reappearance of the supernatural, a dance, a brawl). When Act IV of *Hamlet* starts, the play's supernatural element has already re-appeared (at the end of III.iv); the element of spectacle here involves the disintegration of Ophelia's sanity. And although technically this act does delay the final confrontation between Hamlet and Claudius, the pace accelerates rapidly as all of the pieces (including several we've not seen in a while) move toward the end-game.

Echoes

Act IV contains several echoes to earlier acts. Even minor moments like Polonius noting that Laertes's ship was waiting for him receive an echo here, in Claudius's words to Hamlet. These structural reminders are mnemonic, useful for intensifying the drama so that when it finally explodes in V.ii, it does so with the full force and nuance of the entire play behind it.

Study Guide and Questions, IV.i

1. Summarize what happens in IV.i. Who learns what from whom, and what's the plan?

2. The caesura in IV.i.3 can't belong to Claudius; it's Gertrude's. Why, and what happens in that silence?

3. What does this mean: "Mad as the sea and wind when both contend/ Which is the mightier" (IV.i.7-8)?

4. Why is it particularly apt that Gertrude describe Hamlet's madness both in terms of natural forces *(see Question #3)* and in terms of a failure of reason ("brainish apprehension" [IV.i.11])?

5. Claudius's first thought upon hearing of Hamlet's crime is given in line 13. Do you doubt the truth of this line? How does Gertrude hear it? Is it a confession?

6. At line 15, another list of three. Which object of harm is presented as rhetorically the most important? Do you believe Claudius here? If not, what is he doing and why?

7. The metaphor of feeding/disease/rot is back in Claudius's speech. According to Claudius, whose fault is the spread of this disease? What explanation does he provide for allowing that disease to spread? How is he both telling the truth and not telling the truth in that explanation?

Study Guide and Questions, IV.ii

1. To what does Hamlet's first line refer?

2. Rosencrantz's first line (IV.ii.5) has a feminine ending. Please explore at least three different weaknesses (of differing specificity and scope) that may be invoked by the word itself ("body").

3. Hamlet's response to Rosencrantz (IV.ii.6) echoes what line often spoken at funerals?

4. Explore how this line (still on IV.ii.6) provides a distant echo of and expands Hamlet's first line in the entire play. (Bonus points for providing Claudius's recent line that makes the echo quite timely.)

5. What does Rosencrantz literally mean by "thence" (IV.ii.7)?

6. In IV.ii.9, Hamlet's use of the indefinite pronoun ("it") can refer to any one of (or many of) several things.

    a. If Hamlet's "it" shares the referent for Rosencrantz's "it," what is "it"? In which case, what might Hamlet mean by "Do not believe it"?

    b. If Hamlet's "it" uses Rosencrantz's last word, "chapel," as its referent, what might Hamlet mean by "Do not believe it"?

    c. If Hamlet's "it" refers to something else altogether— not grammatically, but in the scope of his own mind, something he doesn't say and that Rosencrantz doesn't hear, what might "it" be, and what might he then mean by "Do not believe it"?

7. How does Hamlet identify himself in IV.ii.14, and why is he finally, finally able to do so?

8. Bevington's footnote to lines 28-29 provides one way to read those lines. What (or who else) might Hamlet mean by "The body is with the King" in line 28?

9. For such a short scene, this one switches back and forth from prose to blank verse to prose again with lightning speed. Give the line number where it switches from prose to blank verse and the line number where it switches back again, and explain how and why both shifts are perfectly appropriate according to dramatic convention. *(Hint: Pay attention to which characters' lines govern the shift.)*

Study Guide and Questions, IV.iii

1. In the scene's opening lines, what public reason does Claudius give his attendants for not coming down on Hamlet with the full force of the law?

2. How does Claudius insult the groundlings during his explanation of that reason?

3. What is the commonplace wisdom Claudius invokes in IV.iii.9-11? *(Hint: it, too, relies on the repetition of the word "desperate.")*

4. Consider and justify the use of stichomythia in line 13.

5. Explain the truth of Hamlet's first response to Claudius ("At supper" [IV.iii.17]).

6. Hamlet's lines at IV.iii.34-36 explicitly invoke propositional logic: IF your messenger find him not there, [THEN] seek him i'th'other place yourself. Continue this logic: GIVEN that neither Hamlet nor Claudius believes that Heaven was Polonius's likely destination, THEREFORE Hamlet is telling Claudius to do what?

7. Hamlet's continuation in IV.iii.36-38, which contains yet another propositional logic statement, provides the actual location for Polonius's body. Why is it appropriate for Hamlet to answer the question "Where's Polonius?" with two truths—one regarding his soul, one his body? In other words, how does this double truth invoke Hamlet's central problem from the beginning of the play as it has developed thus far?

8. What reason does Claudius give Hamlet for not coming down on him with the full force of the law? Provide the quotation, the citation, and a restatement in contemporary, nuanced language.

9. Lines 53-56 repeat the words that bear the full weight of the emotional motivations for both characters: mother, father, wife.

   a. What does Hamlet mean by calling Claudius his mother? What does Claudius mean by correcting Hamlet with "Your loving father"?

   b. Why does Claudius do that now, when both characters know exactly who Hamlet's actual loving father was?

   c. Micro-structural read: So far, Claudius has stated two reasons for sending Hamlet to England (rather than having him executed for murder); how does this moment inadvertently provide the missing third reason and attest to its probable importance?

10. How does the Hamlet/Claudius exchange echo:

   a. Claudius's first exchange with Laertes?

   b. Claudius's first exchange with Hamlet?

   c. Polonius's first exchange with Laertes?

11. Claudius tells England to kill Hamlet, then alludes to "the hectic in my blood" (IV.iii.70). What's being echoed remarkably specifically with that phrase?

Study Guide and Questions, IV.iv

Shakespeare's next few scenes indicate "traveling" very cleverly, despite occurring on a static stage. Watch for how.

1. This scene includes multiple characters traveling to different locations. Explain precisely how Shakespeare accomplishes this on a very small stage by thoroughly listing who appears with whom, who stays, who exits, where they're going, and why, who enters next, etc., until you end with Hamlet alone on stage.

2. What, precisely, is the Captain's opinion of the value of the war against Poland?

3. How does Hamlet turn this opinion inward, and toward what end?

4. Explain the feminine ending in IV.iv.33.

5. In line IV.iv.36, -37, and -39, Hamlet's wording indicates that he may now identify with his mother (you will need to recall the specific language he uses in his first soliloquy [I.ii.129-159]), although not in a good way. How?

6. At lines IV.iv.47-66, Hamlet very precisely echoes the language of another of his earlier soliloquies. Which? How? And where?

7. You could easily argue that the soliloquy that ends IV.iv is Hamlet's absolute lowest point in the play so far, yet— weirdly, for those who choose to play Hamlet as suicidal— he's not thinking at all about suicide here.

   a. Why not (from a character standpoint)?

b. Why from a structural standpoint does suicide become a present absence here, its temporary lack fulfilled through juxtaposition with the focus of the next scene (IV.v)? *(Suggestion: Finish the rest of the questions for this act before responding to this question.)*

Study Guide and Questions, IV.v

1. The scene opens with Hamlet's greatest ally, Horatio, in the company of Hamlet's biggest problem, Gertrude, and a random gentleman (who exists to provide a bit of information). Why might Shakespeare want to put Gertrude in Horatio's company at this precise moment in the play? *(Hint: Remember when last we saw her.)*

2. Gertrude's first line is shocking. How? Why might she feel this way right now? How does this line indicate a choice that may provide an answer to a really big question regarding her character, her priorities?

3. Explain the feminine ending in IV.v.2.

4. Gertrude speaks the entirety of the opening of this scene in single syllable words. Why?

5. What is the first word she utters in this scene that contains more than one syllable (provide the word and the citation)? Why that word?

6. The gentleman's speech to Gertrude indicates that Ophelia's nonsense (or half-sense) nonetheless moves those who hear it to inferring meaning, elevating that inferred meaning to the status of truth. This connects to the play's larger issue that people, when given only partial information, reflexively attempt to provide full meaning, making it up if they have to. How might hearing this fulfill the Ghost's injunction to Hamlet to leave Gertrude to her own conscience?

7. Continuing from Question #6, how might hearing this make Gertrude feel pride in her son?

8. Explain the rhyming couplet in IV.v.19-20, both denotatively (restate these lines in contemporary, nuanced language) and in terms of why we might get a rhyming couplet here, in the middle of a scene.

9. IV.v.19-20 contain pretty much all we're going to get from Gertrude regarding whether or not she has chosen to believe in/trust/hold faith with Hamlet between their intense confrontation in III.iv and the final showdown in V.ii, which will take place in front of the entire court and thus involve potential "seeming" versus full expression of authenticity. Based on IV.v.19-20, has Gertrude chosen to hold faith with Hamlet or not? Explain with reference to what she says in those lines.

10. Ophelia's first line in this scene (IV.v.21) asks where the "beauteous majesty of Denmark" is. What are several things she might mean by that phrase?

11. Claudius's first line in this scene contains at least a double meaning. Identify both, and explain how both contain truth.

12. At IV.v.75, Claudius makes a request of Horatio, and Horatio immediately fulfills it. This echoes an earlier moment when Claudius seemed to "request" something of Hamlet's friends Rosencrantz and Guildenstern. Remember that Horatio is not Danish, not a subject of Claudius, and thus risks no treason should he decide not to comply. Although Horatio says nothing, he complies. Why does he (list at least three reasons)? And how do you know how to read this silence?

13. In Claudius's speech to Gertrude, in which he lists all of the ills that have befallen Denmark recently, he uses several

words that have featured prominently in his earlier speeches and actions. Locate at least two, and explore why Shakespeare may have chosen to use them here.

14. Treason! Claudius learns that Laertes has sparked a mutiny and is coming for Claudius. What does Laertes think has happened, and to whom are we supposed to compare him in this moment? (Not Shakespeare at his most subtle, this time...)

15. In the exchange that follows between Claudius and Laertes, Shakespeare provides touchstones for three aspects of the same issue that has plagued Hamlet since Act I.

    a. Render lines IV.v.121-24 in contemporary, nuanced language, and explain how Laertes's words touch on Hamlet's dilemma.

    b. Line IV.v.136 opens with another echo of Hamlet's dilemma; explain.

    c. Claudius's questions at lines IV.v.146-47 and -149 provide a third touchstone; explain. Bonus: Explain how IV.v.149 is especially ironic.

16. At lines IV.v.147-49, there are three caesurae which seem to belong to Laertes's character. What is it that is slowing the pace here, given his bursting in ready to kill anyone and everything?

17. At line IV.v.178, Laertes's line linguistically echoes Gertrude's earlier irritation with Polonius (II.ii.95). Explore how Leartes's line is an inversion of Gertrude's, and what truth it contains that might have mattered centrally to Shakespeare. (*Hint: consider how "art" may be considered "nothing."*)

18. Using the footnotes, be the director for Ophelia's flower distribution in lines 179-89. To whom does she present each flower, and why? Explore possibilities, but in the end, you have to tell your actor your final decisions.

19. Although Claudius isn't lying about having had no literal hand in Polonius's death, his rhetorical list-of-three at IV.iv.210-11 may (or may not) indicate that he's lying here. If he is lying, how does that list reveal it? If he's not lying, what has changed, and why?

20. Laertes is angry about a lot, here, and justifiably; in IV.v.216-19, he (like his father before him) spends rather more lines than one might expect on one of them. In addition to his father's death and his sister's ensuing madness, these lines indicate that which abstract value is also important enough to him to have risked treason, death, and damnation for it?

21. As this scene ends, Claudius provides an almost perfect echo for another character's actions at the close of an earlier scene. Which character, how, and what's Shakespeare's possible purpose in providing that echo at this moment?

Study Guide and Questions, IV.vi

1. What is the gist of the letter Horatio receives from Hamlet?

2. What does Horatio ask of the First Sailor?

3. Why does this scene end without a rhyming couplet?

Study Guide and Questions, IV.vii

1. In the opening lines (IV.vii.1-5), Claudius presents his earlier assumption to Laertes as though it is truth—why does it cost Claudius nothing to share this truth with Laertes?

2. What purpose does the word "ear" serve for the audience in line 3?

3. Laertes's response touches on "seeming v. being." How? What kind of evidence does Laertes ask for (IV.vii.5-9) to satisfy his conscience? *(Note: Not what evidence; what kind of evidence.)*

4. In IV.vii.10-25, Claudius provides two answers to Laertes's question. What are they, simply put?

5. What happens in the caesura in IV.vii.10?

6. Explain the feminine ending in IV.vii.11.

7. Claudius is about to say something very predictable to Laertes in IV.vii.36, but he is interrupted. What is the gist of what he was about to say?

8. Of the two letters the Messenger brings, we hear one. Why does Claudius find its postscript especially unsettling?

9. Why does Shakespeare leave the other letter unread/unheard?

10. In the exchange from IV.vii.71-106, on what grounds does Claudius propose to manipulate Hamlet into a duel with Laertes? Logic? What kind? Love? Duty? Something else? What? What will make this duel so attractive to Hamlet?

11. Backing up, what makes this solution so attractive to Claudius? The answer is given in two lines (before line 71); find them, quote them, and provide the formal citation.

12. IV.vii.140-41: Explain the stichomythia, and explore how that sets up Laertes's extension of Claudius's plan.

13. Claudius seems especially cautious in IV.vii.149-63, and outlines a back-up plan in case their original "did blast in proof" (IV.vii.155). Although Bevington provides the footnote ("blast in proof" = "come to grief when put to the test"—in other words, in case the plan doesn't work), Shakespeare's use of the word "proof" could use some exploration here. Why use that particular word right now?

14. In IV.vii.167-184, Gertrude shares the unhappy news of Ophelia's death.

    a. What exactly was Ophelia doing that caused her to tumble into the brook? What happened to her then?

    b. If Shakespeare is echoing an earlier, abstract critique on Elizabethan gender roles here, locate that critique in the play and provide the full text of relevant passage(s), with formal citation.

    c. How might what happened to Ophelia render that earlier conceptual critique literal?

15. Why does this scene (and thus this entire act) end without a rhyming couplet?

Act V

Study Guide and Questions: Act V

Clowns

To elaborate on Bevington's footnote regarding "Clowns": Please forget everything you know about circus clowns; in this context and at this time, "clowns" are "rustics" or "peasants" or "extremely lower-class characters" who, still in this context, provide a bit of (needed but pointed) comic relief. They are not meant to be slapstick characters, exactly; they function like fools and madmen in Shakespeare's plays—they can speak the uncomfortable truth because of distance from social power.

This distance is provided variously by social function (court jesters, who could—within limits—poke fun at kings and courtly counselors), insanity (a sane Ophelia cannot sing raunchy songs; an insane Ophelia can), or social class. They served the same function on the Elizabethan stage as children sometimes do now. The contemporary saying "Out of the mouths of babes" comes very close—children can, by virtue of not being fully indoctrinated into social niceties, get away with speaking truths that every adult present knows but is trying not to mention. Jesters, lunatics, drunks, and lower-class characters (when alone) voice such truths for Shakespeare's original audience. Classist? Perhaps, but Elizabethan England was a class-conscious world.

Study Guide and Questions, V.i

1. Why are the Clowns speaking in prose?

2. Why is there a question as to the appropriate site of Ophelia's burial?

3. The Second Clown overtly addresses social class inequality within the opening pages of the Act. Provide the full quotation and the formal citation.

4. Social class commentary continues. By what logic does the First Clown conclude the primacy of their profession over the church? Provide the full quotation and the formal citation.

5. More with social class. Hamlet is shocked to hear a gravedigger singing. Explain Horatio's response.

6. "The hand of little employment hath the daintier sense" (V.i.70). Explain.

7. Hamlet and Horatio are also speaking in prose. A fast answer to the "Why" is that they're good friends, but they're also on stage with lower class characters. Account for that anomaly.

8. First Clown tosses a skull he's found, and Hamlet ruminates at some length on his surprise. What is the gist of Hamlet's overall response (contained in lines 75-116)? Sum it up in a couple of sentences. Try not to lose nuance when you do.

9. Line 119 contain an example of sophomoric logic. How so? Explain. *(Hint: Etymologically, "sophomore" means "wise fool.")*

10. Hamlet and the First Clown have a long dialogue in prose. How can this be justified given that: no one is drunk, no one is pretending to be insane, no one is actually insane, they do not share a social class, and they are not friends?

11. Hamlet's famous line "Alas, poor Yorick!" initiates further commentary on death. Explain what he means by "Now get you to my lady's chamber and tell her, let her paint an inch thick, to this favor she must come. Let her laugh at that" (V.i.192-94).

12. For once, Horatio advises Hamlet to perhaps stop pursuing a particular line of thought (V.i.205). He may be speaking lightheartedly and jokingly; he may be absolutely serious; he might be speaking half in jest in full earnest. Why might he advise his friend to stop pursuing that line of thought? (The answer is not in the text.)

13. In the middle of Hamlet's next speech (V.i.207-16), he switches back into verse. This is before the entrance of the royal court, so that's not the reason. Look closely at the lines in verse and see if you can tease out evidence for a reason for the form switch. *(Hint: How do those lines work? What do they contain? Spot a poetic feature and see if you can connect these particular lines in this particular moment to the more usual circumstances for that particular poetic feature.)*

14. Hamlet is able to tell from the appearance of the funeral procession that the corpse is that of a suicide and of some rank. Although we're not given any of the evidence for how he knows this, we know without doubt what kind of logic he's employed to reach his conclusions. What kind?

15. Why might Shakespeare want in this moment to remind us of the power of Hamlet's mind?

16. The Priest notes that the questions surrounding Ophelia's death prescribe that she not be allowed certain burial rites. List them.

17. The Priest notes that usual church practice has been overruled "by great command." In all likelihood, whose?

18. Connect your response to Question #17 to III.iii.

19. What happens in the caesura in line 234? *(Note: It is emphatically not a physical action.)*

20. Laertes's curse on the person responsible for Ophelia's death could as easily have been said by Gertrude to Claudius about her son. How so?

21. Laertes's passion of grief causes him to leap into Ophelia's open grave with her. The text indicates that this stage direction was provided by the editor. How do you know?

22. Why did the editor put that stage direction specifically right there?

23. Laertes then fights with Hamlet. What are some of the specific moves fight choreographers must include in their design for this fight? Provide the evidence.

24. In lines 262-64, Hamlet overtly acknowledges the foil relationship he and Laertes share. How, precisely?

25. Hamlet's earlier line "For I have that within which passes show" (I.ii.85) receives an echo and an evolution in lines 260-62. Where, precisely? Why might Shakespeare have chosen this moment to echo the earlier one?

26. Based on Question #25: How has Hamlet's innate character stayed the same since Act I? How has it evolved?

27. Consider lines 269-75: The exchange among Gertrude, Hamlet, and Claudius provides an ironic affirmation of what was unquestionably a flaw in Polonius's overarching logic. How?

28. When Gertrude says, "For love of God, forbear him" (V.i.276), to whom is she speaking? About whom? She might be speaking to someone else; who? In which case, about whom? (More ambiguity to Gertrude, more often.)

29. Claudius is the one who now must wait and bide his time, just as Hamlet did until III.ii. Provide the exact quotation that indicates this (with formal citation).

30. The speech that closes the scene repeats the word "patience." Shakespeare could easily have avoided that repetition; why is Claudius repeating the word "patience" here? Answer for every level:

    a. As he speaks to himself.

    b. As he speaks to Laertes.

    c. As he speaks to Gertrude.

    d. As the play speaks to the groundlings. (What is Shakespeare saying to them?)

    e. As the play speaks to its more educated audience. (What is Shakespeare saying to them?)

Questions 31-33: Please provide the full scansion for the following lines and consider possible meanings for poetic devices (metrical substitutions, alliteration, assonance, etc.).

31. Priest: Lines 226-230

32. Laertes: Lines 246-250

33. Hamlet: Lines 272-274

Study Guide and Questions, V.ii

This final scene opens with Hamlet's explanation to Horatio of what happened while he was away. Please provide close-to-the-original prose restatements (using nuanced, contemporary English) of the following lines:

1. "Our indiscretion sometimes serves us well"

2. "When our deep plots do pall"

3. "and that should learn us"

4. "There's a divinity that shapes our ends,/ Rough hew them how we will—"

5. "Being thus benetted round with villainies—"

6. "Ere I could make a prologue to my brains,/ They had begun the play—"

7. "I sat me down/ Devised a new commission, wrote it fair."

8. "I once did hold it, as our statists do,/ A baseness to write fair, and labored much/ How to forget that learning"

9. "... on the view and knowing of these contents"

10. "Without debatement further more or less"

11. "He should those bearers put to sudden death,/ Not shriving time allowed."

12. "... they did make love to this employment."

13. "They are not near my conscience."

14. "Their defeat/ Does by their own insinuation grow."

15. "'Tis dangerous when the baser nature comes/ Between the pass and fell incensèd points/ Of mighty opposites."

16. Which of the lines provided in Questions #1-15 specifically allude to Hamlet's previous use of propositional logic? How?

17. Which of the lines provided in Questions #1-15 specifically allude to Hamlet's elaborate machinations regarding *The Murder of Gonzago*? How?

18. Which of the lines provided in Questions #1-15 specifically allude to Claudius's murder of King Hamlet? How?

19. Pertaining to lines 75-80: What does Hamlet mean by "For by the image of my cause I see/ The portraiture of his"?

20. Still with the same lines, what reason does Hamlet give for his brawl with Laertes?

21. Upon the entrance of Osric, the scene switches to prose. Osric's social status is unquestionably lower than Hamlet's (whose isn't, at this point, really...)—and although Hamlet and Horatio's close friendship can sometimes warrant prose, neither of them is friends with Osric. Please posit a theory and justification for why this scene happens in prose.

22. What are the terms of Claudius's wager with Laertes as reported by Osric in lines 146-52 and 163-64? Please restate them using propositional logic form.

23. We were set up for this moment in I.v, with Hamlet's line, "There are more things in heaven and earth, Horatio,/ than are dreamt of in your philosophy" (175-76). Given that the

study of philosophy at the time was the study of propositional logic in service of theology, what do you make of Shakespeare's pointing out at this moment, just before the climactic fight, that all propositional logic can be compared to a kind of gamble?

24. We learn somewhat randomly that Hamlet's been constantly practicing sword fighting since Laertes went to France. This is the Elizabethan equivalent of going to the gym. What insight does this give us into his character? (You may, if you wish, consider the emotions we know Hamlet's been feeling but that we and the court have not been seeing.)

25. Find the line at which Laertes makes his final choice between love and duty. Which does he choose? Provide the full quotation and the formal citation; explain your choice.

26. Same as Question #25, for Horatio.

27. Same as Question #25, for Gertrude.

28. How is "He has my dying voice" (V.ii.358) an act of kingship?

29. Regarding Hamlet's last line in the play:

    a. How and why is it particularly apt that Hamlet's last line be "The rest is silence"?

    b. Propose three separate and distinct possible reasons (it's okay if they're contradictory) for the feminine ending and briefly explain why each might apply.

30. Staging: Arrange the tableau of the stage at Horatio's lines 361-62. You must account for the position of all the characters on stage whether alive or dead, including any

non-speaking characters whose presence is required for stage business, as well as the position of the throne of Denmark. Draw this as well as you can, and label each character and body.

31. And finally: Justify your choice regarding whose body, if anyone's, occupies the physical throne in this tableau.

Projects

Culminating Projects

Option I: The Royal Medical Examiner

By Command of His Royal Majesty, Fortinbras I, Soon-to-be-Crowned King of Denmark:

Thou art appointed medical examiner to Our court.

It has come to Our attention that yon throne room be a bit bloody, and We yearn to know the reasons behind this. Before We set the castle cleaning wenches and able-bodied drudges to their daunting task of tidying up a bit in preparation for Our coronation, We command the following:

1. Provide Us with a body count tallying the deaths fallen upon this fair kingdom and/or upon such citizens thereof noted in the passages recounted to Us by William Shakespeare (with the assistance of Horatio, friend and advisor to Hamlet-the-Last of the Danish line) as have occurred starting with the Death of the Late King Hamlet the Elder, brother to the Late King Claudius and father of the Late King Hamlet the Last.

2. As part of this body count, please provide the following information:

    a. Name and full rank (if any) of deceased

    b. Medical cause(s) of death (see 2.f.)

    c. Person or persons physically responsible for said death (see 2.f.)

    d. Person or persons morally responsible for said death (see 2.f.)

    e. Thoughtful, thorough, and complete explanatory proof of said moral culpability, including…

    f. … one or two direct, formally cited quotations indicating where you locate your evidence for 2.b., 2.c., and 2.d.—one or two quotations for each part (b, c, and d). You must name the character who speaks the lines you quote as well.

3. Format: You may submit your report to Us in any number of material formats. As the digital age is still several centuries hence, We do not accept reports in formats beyond our technological capabilities. You may have them delivered by Fruit Peddlers (precursors to Apple products), Fenestral Projectile (precursors to Apple competitors), or Dunce Carts (precursors to Smart Phones). We shall be pleased to accept traditional double-spaced scrolls, spreadsheet parchments, or individually designed death certificates suitable for framing and display in the Hall of History, which We shall dedicate to the memory of these troubled times here in Our Castle Elsinore.

It is so commanded.

~ Fortinbras I of Denmark, Crown Prince of Norway

Option II: Private Papers:
A Diary plus Other Documents

By order of the Medical Examiner of the Court of Denmark at the Behest of His Royal Majesty, Fortinbras I:

To the Castle's Cleaning Wenches and Able-Bodied Drudges:

Any and all private papers belonging to any lately deceased members of the Court, their families, or their servants must be delivered to me in the Office of the Castle Seneschal.

Of particular requirement are diaries (plus any additional papers) belonging to:

Ghost of Hamlet-the-Elder*

Hamlet, Crown Prince and Uncrowned King of Denmark

Claudius, King of Denmark ("the Vile")

Gertrude, Queen of Denmark ("the Cruel" ~or~ "the Unfortunate" ~or~ "the Addlepated")

The lady Ophelia (Later: the Madwoman of Elsinore)*

His Excellency Polonius the Over-reaching*

Horatio the Scholar

Goodman Schmidt the Butler**

Goodwife Iona the Housekeeper**

---

*Assume that all deaths result in ghosts and that all ghosts have an unbridled urge to keep writing in their diaries post-mortem. Whether death alters the format of diaries is entirely up to your imagination.

**Imaginary head servants, just in case you'd enjoy writing from a servant's perspective—because why should the upper classes have all the fun? Assume the servants survive into Fortinbras I's reign.

Pick one of the above characters and provide the contents of his/her diary beginning with the death of Hamlet, Sr., and continuing through the end of the play—one entry per scene in the play (clearly marked as such), whether or not that character is present in the scene—assume that Elsinore's servants gossip like blazes so every character knows at least the surface of plot events they don't personally witness.

Any additional papers (letters, bad poetry, good poetry, unpaid bills, instructions to servants, designs for new clothes, military tactical maps, favorite quotations, confessional ravings, prayer drafts, doodles) you think might be found strewn about or hidden in those characters' private chambers can of course be included; use your imagination.

General Advice: Have fun.

Glossary

Glossary

Alliteration/Alliterative Repeated consonant sounds. *(See also: Assonance.)*

Amphibrach/Amphibrachic A trisyllabic metric foot with the stress pattern (u / u). The name "Joanna" is an amphibrach; the amphibrach is the first foot in a limerick ("There **once** was | a **stone** in | my **shoe**.") *(See also: Metric Foot; Scansion; Substitution.)*

Anapest/Anapestic A trisyllabic metric foot with the stress pattern (u u /). The word "afternoon" is an anapest. *(See also: Metric Foot; Scansion; Substitution)*

Antithesis/Antithetical A syntactically exact compressed playing off of opposites creating an echo effect, inviting readers to compare parallel words. The longer the antithetical elements, the less exact the syntactic echo need be.

Example 1 (syntactically exact):

> Queen: Hamlet, thou hast thy father much offended.
> Hamlet: Mother, you have my father much offended.

The lines are antithetical and the syntactic echo is exact:

> Gertrude: [address][informal pron.][verb][poss. pron.][adv.][adj.]
> Hamlet:　[address][formal pron.]　[verb][poss. pron.][adv.][adj.]

The "opposites" are subtle—Hamlet sets "Mother" up in opposition to himself ("Hamlet") and changes the second-person pronoun from informal ("thou") to the formal ("you"). Subtle but powerful, Hamlet is furious, and this III.iv confrontation has been coming since I.ii (and building for months before that).

Example 2 (syntactically inexact):

> Richard: Never came poison from so sweet a place.
> Anne: Never hung poison on a fouler toad.
>
> (*Richard III*, II.i.146-147)

The syntax isn't exact, but it's close enough for an echo effect:

> Richard: [adv.][verb][noun][prep.][adv.][adj.][article][noun].
> Anne: [adv.][verb][noun][prep.]   [article][adj.][noun].

The opposition is less subtle (and these two verbal combatants less evenly matched, perhaps): the "sweet place" is Anne's lips (she has just spit at Richard); the opposition is the "toad" (Richard). Ironically, this princess will kiss (marry) this frog. It will, predictably, not go well.

Assonance/Assonant Repeated vowel sounds. *(See also: Alliteration.)*

Bacchius/Bacchic A trisyllabic metric foot with the stress pattern (u / /). The word "martini" can be bacchic. *(See also: Metric Foot; Scansion; Substitution.)*

Blank Verse Unrhymed iambic pentameter. This is the general baseline of Shakespeare's language in the plays; the language doesn't strictly adhere to this (that would be boring), but this is the standard from which students of Shakespeare's language measure departures and variants. *(See also: Iambic Pentameter; Prose.)*

Caesura (plural: caesurae) In blank verse, when a line has fewer than ten syllables and the next line begins again at the left margin, the resultant beat or two of silence. Something happens in Shakespeare's caesurae; it's up to the reader/actor/director to determine what may or must happen—some movement, an entrance, a gesture, a look, a thought, a decision, etc. *(See also: Stichomythia.)*

Citation Quotations from Shakespeare are cited by act, scene, and line number(s) as given in the following example: "How cheerfully on the false trail they cry!" (IV.v.112). Multiple lines include a slash between lines and numbers are hyphenated as follows: "How came he dear? I'll not be juggled with. / To hell, allegiance! Vows, to the blackest devil!" (IV.v.133-4).

Conceit An extended metaphor. Claudius identifies Ophelia's songs and non sequiturs as "Conceit on her father" (IV.v.45).

Cretic/Cretic A trisyllabic metric foot with the stress pattern (/ u /). The command "Go away" is cretic. *(See also: Metric Foot; Scansion; Substitution.)*

Dactyl/Dactylic A trisyllabic metric foot with the stress pattern (/ u u). "Dactyl" is from the Greek word for for "finger"; the stress pattern mimics the distances between finger joints (long, short, short). The word "anyway" is dactylic. *(See also: Metric Foot; Scansion; Substitution.)*

Dialogue/Dialogic The baseline form of the text in Shakespeare's plays. Self-explanatory; multiple characters conversing. *(See also: Monologue; Soliloquy.)*

Disyllable/Disyllabic A metric foot comprised of two syllables. *(See also: Meter; Metric Foot; Scansion; Trisyllable.)*

Dramatic Irony Occurs when the audience knows something a character or group of characters doesn't. Can also occur when some but not all characters on stage share the audience's knowledge. Example: The moment in a horror movie when the audience thinks, "Don't go outside!" Not to be confused with irony or situational irony.

End-stopped A line of verse that ends with a comma, period, or other punctuation. Can indicate several things—emotional intensity; that a character is unsettled by something; that a character is talking down to someone. It usually indicates either that a usually eloquent and/or intelligent character is temporarily destabilized or that the character might not be very eloquent generally—compare to the character's lines elsewhere in the play to establish which. *(See also: Enjambment.)*

Enjambment/Enjambed When a line of verse does not end with a comma, period, or other punctuation but continues directly into the next line, these lines are said to be "enjambed." Characters whose lines display consistent frequent enjambment throughout an entire play are generally considered extremely intelligent. The opposite is not necessarily true; lack of enjambment does not necessarily mean that a character is unintelligent. *(See also: End-stopped.)*

Exact Rhyme Self-explanatory—the rhyme is exact: cat/hat; through/blue.

Feminine Ending In blank verse, a line having eleven syllables with the final syllable unstressed is said to have a "feminine ending." Gender equity issues aside (the name is fairly old), lines with feminine endings indicate that some weakness is lurking in the vicinity of the line. Whether the character is identifying a weakness in him- or herself, in what he or she is talking about, in his or her present situation, or in a concept at play in the line varies and depends on denotative meaning and dramatic context. The unstressed eleventh syllable is a clue to the reader/actor to consider how "weakness" may be at play in that particular word, line, or moment. *(See extended example from* Macbeth *on pages 32-34 of the Drama, Language, and Aurality section of this guide.)*

Foils/Foil Relationships When two characters, pairs of characters, or situations bear multiple strong similarities, they are said to be foils of each other or to exist in a foil relationship. Foil relationships allow a reader to isolate a difference—usually a single one—that conventionally accounts for and allows for deeper thinking on the effects of that single difference. For example, Hamlet, Sr., (the Ghost) and Claudius constitute an obvious foil relationship: They are brothers, both Kings of Denmark, both husbands of Gertrude, and they even look somewhat alike. However, one is Hamlet's father, and one is not, and thereon hangs an entire play.

Pairs of characters can also exist in foil relationships; Cornelius and Voltimand may be considered foils for Rosencrantz and Guildenstern—not individually, but collectively. Larger groups, especially families, countries, and situations also offer foils. For example, the royal houses of Denmark and Norway are foils for each other; in both houses, the first Kings are now deceased; both Kings share names with their surviving sons; their brothers, both in some way "sick" or "diseased," now sit on the thrones. The salient difference is that whereas the royal house of Norway mentions no mother/wife/queen, the royal house of Denmark most emphatically does. This is Shakespeare's way of subtly underscoring Gertrude's centrality (at least emotional centrality) to the play.

Formal Citation (*See **Citation***)

Iamb/Iambic A disyllabic metric foot with the stress pattern (u /). The word "until" is iambic. (*See also: Metric Foot; Scansion; Substitution.*)

Iambic Pentameter The baseline metric pattern for Shakespeare's plays: ten-syllable lines each consisting of five iambs. (Iambs are two syllables; "penta-" = five; 2 x 5 = 10). Given that an iamb contains an unstressed syllable (u) followed by a stressed syllable (/), the rhythm (meter) of a line of iambic pentameter is:

$$u / u / u / u / u /$$

The name "Marie" is an iamb; say the name aloud five times ("Marie Marie Marie Marie Marie") to hear the rhythmic (metric) pattern of iambic pentameter. (*See also: Blank Verse; Iambic Tetrameter.*)

Iambic Tetrameter The metric pattern used in Shakespeare by witches, elementals, fairies (sometimes), and other supernatural creatures; also, in songs, no matter who is singing them. Eight-syllable lines consisting of four iambs. (Iambs are two syllables;

"tetra-" = four; 2 x 4 = 8). Given that an iamb contains an unstressed syllable (u) followed by a stressed syllable (/), the rhythm (meter) of a line of iambic tetrameter is:

u / u / u / u /

Say the name "Marie" (an iamb) aloud four times to hear the metric pattern of iambic tetrameter. Examples: "A foolish thing was but a toy" (Feste's song, *Twelfth Night* [V.i.391]); "Full fathom five thy father lies" (Ariel's song, *The Tempest* [I.ii.400]). *(See also: Iambic Pentameter.)*

Internal Rhyme When a rhyme occurs not at the end of a line but somewhere in the middle, it's called an internal rhyme.

Irony/Ironic When the words spoken are the literal opposite of the speaker's meaning. *(See also: Dramatic Irony; Situational Irony.)*

Line Rubric Stage direction provided in a character's spoken line(s) (as opposed to in parentheses or italics, as other stage directions are; most of these others are editorial interventions and not original to Shakespeare; Shakespeare's most famous original stage direction is from *The Winter's Tale*: Exit, pursued by a bear). Example: "Here, Hamlet, take my napkin, rub thy brows" (V.ii.290).

Metaphor/Metaphorical A form of figurative language; a comparison drawn without using "like" or "as." *(See also: Conceit; Simile.)*

Meter/Metric Rhythm in poetry; a particular form of poetic rhythm. Can refer to the rhythm of a single line or the baseline rhythm from which Shakespeare departs slightly or drastically to achieve particular emphasis. The baseline meter of Shakespeare is iambic pentameter.

Metric Foot The smallest element of poetic rhythm, either disyllabic (two syllables) or trisyllabic (three syllables). Shakespeare's baseline foot is the disyllabic iamb. *(See also: Scansion; Substitution.)*

Molossus/Molossic A trisyllabic metric foot with the stress pattern (/ / /). Any three-syllable name shouted to get someone's attention (*e.g.,* "EMILY!") is molossic. *(See also: Metric Foot; Scansion; Substitution.)*

Monologue/Monologic A longish speech by a character when other characters are present. Characters delivering monologues may be knowingly lying/spinning the truth. *(See also: Soliloquy.)*

Near Rhyme: A rhyme that is close, but not exact. Example: mourn/before. Near rhymes depend on assonance.

Onomatopoeia/onomatopoeic: A word that sounds like what it is (*e.g.,* crunch, smash, shatter, etc.).

Poetic Contraction A contraction made when omitting a syllable to preserve meter. Example: "O'er" for "over."

Prose Self-explanatory; evident by an even right-hand margin. If Shakespearean characters are speaking in prose, generally one of three things is happening:

> a. There are only lower-class characters on-stage

> b. The character speaking in prose is insane…

> c. … or is pretending to be.

Good friends in the upper classes (*e.g.,* Hamlet and Horatio) will sometimes (rarely) switch into prose when they are alone.

Pyrrhus/Pyrrhic A disyllabic metric foot with the stress pattern (u u). This usually occurs when two unstressed syllables from longer polysyllabic words occur in a line such that they comprise a foot in themselves. Example: The middle two syllables of "Always between" could comprise a pyrrhic foot: **Al**- |ways be- | **tween**. *(See also: Metric Foot; Scansion; Substitution; Tribrach.)*

Rhyming Couplet In blank verse, two adjacent lines that rhyme comprise a rhyming couplet. Often used to indicate scene endings as it provides an aural cue to the actors waiting to come on stage to begin the next scene. It functions as a bit of a "button" to the scene, as well. Example: "More relative than this. The play's the thing / Wherein I'll catch the conscience of the King" (II.ii.605-6). (There are other times Shakespeare uses rhyming couplets; these are generally easy to spot and their function to deduce from context.)

Scansion The inexact art and science of metric analysis whereby substitutions are identified and possible variants are explored. *(See also: Metric Foot; Substitution.)*

Simile A comparison drawn using "like" or "as." *(See also: Conceit; Metaphor.)*

Situational Irony When events result which are the opposite of what was intended or expected. *(See also: Dramatic Irony; Irony.)*

Spondee/Spondaic A disyllabic metric foot with the stress pattern (/ /). Any two-syllable name shouted to get someone's attention (*e.g.,* "STELLA!") is spondaic. *(See also: Metric Foot; Scansion; Substitution.)*

Soliloquy A longish speech by a character when no other characters are present. The conventions regarding soliloquies include: they reflect a character's innermost thoughts; the character is addressing the audience. They function a bit like the Chorus in Athenian drama and a bit like voice-overs in television and film. If a character delivers a soliloquy, the convention is that the character believes what s/he is saying—he may be lying to him- or herself, but s/he doesn't realize it. *(See also: Monologue.)*

Stichomythia A fairly frequent form of dialogue in which multiple characters share the 10-syllables of the standard Shakespearean line, indicated by the second speaker's line starting in the middle of the page rather than at the usual left-hand margin. The effect of such moments is rapid-fire; this dialogic form has a specific page layout that indicates that the actors should not pause between each other's lines. Stichomythia is usually reserved for moments of extreme emotional intensity and urgency (anger; excitement) and/or high tension moments (key plot moments). *(See also: Caesura; Dialogue.)*

Substitution In Shakespearean blank verse, any line not consisting of five iambs contains at least one substitution (a non-iambic metric foot). Example:

Now is | the **win**|ter of | our **dis** | content

(Richard III, I.i.1)

The first "foot" ("**Now** is") is a substitution: a trochee (/ u) substituted for iamb.

The second ("the **win**-"), fourth ("our **dis**-"), and fifth ("**content**") feet are iambs (u /)—the "baseline" foot.

The third "foot" ("-ter of") is also a substitution: pyrrhus (u u) substituted for iamb.

The substitutions are exceptional, that is, exceptions to the rule; they vary the "baseline" meter in ways that are audible. Although ten syllables pass very quickly on stage, substitutions provide actors with clues for where to consider the language more closely. What might it mean, for example, for a character to begin a play with a substitution? What might this say about his character's regard for rules, with the law, with God's law? And why the emphasis on the word "Now"? In the remainder of the soliloquy, Richard starts with "Now," delves briefly into the recent past, and then outlines his own villainous plans for the future. So the play starts with the "now," but what is "now" is ephemeral, turning to dust under Richard's machinations. *(See also: Meter; Metric Foot; Scansion.)*

Tribrach/Tribrachic A trisyllabic metric foot with the stress pattern (u u u) . Very rare; usually occurs when three unstressed syllables of two adjacent words comprise a single foot. *(See also: Metric Foot; Pyrrhus; Scansion; Substitution.)*

Trisyllable/Trisyllabic A metric foot comprised of three syllables. *(See also: Disyllable; Meter; Metric Foot; Scansion.)*

Trochee/Trochaic A disyllabic foot with the stress pattern (/ u). The name "Alice" is trochaic. *(See also: Metric Foot; Scansion; Substitution.)*

Turn In Western literature, the turn is the moment at which that which was previously only possible becomes either inevitable or impossible; usually occurs at or near the exact middle of a text (which, in Shakespeare, is often but not always III.ii, thus its alternative name, "the III.ii turn"). The turn in *Hamlet* occurs in III.ii. Prior to Claudius's silent admission of guilt, the question driving the play was "What will Hamlet do?" After that moment, Hamlet's course is obvious: he must try to kill Claudius. After the turn, the question that drives the play is "What will Claudius do?" This structural feature extends far beyond the boundaries of Shakespeare; the turn in the *Harry Potter* series (the middle of which is the fourth book, *Harry Potter and the Goblet of Fire*) is the return of Voldemort to corporeal form, after which a final confrontation between him and Harry isn't just possible, it's inevitable.

Sources

Leon, Donna. *About Face.* New York: Penguin, 2009. Print.

Shakespeare, William. *Hamlet, Prince of Denmark. Four Tragedies: Hamlet, Othello, King Lear, Macbeth.* Eds. David Bevington and David Scott Kastan. New York: Bantam Dell, 2005. 1-274. Print.

---. *Macbeth. The Complete Works of Shakespeare* (Fifth Edition). Ed. David Bevington. New York: Pearson Longman, 2004. 1255-1292. Print.

---. *Romeo and Juliet. The Complete Works of Shakespeare* (Fifth Edition). Ed. David Bevington. New York: Pearson Longman, 2004. 1005-1050. Print.

---. *The Tempest. The Complete Works of Shakespeare* (Fifth Edition). Ed. David Bevington. New York: Pearson Longman, 2004. 1570-1603. Print.

---. *Twelfth Night; Or, What You Will. The Complete Works of Shakespeare* (Fifth Edition). Ed. David Bevington. New York: Pearson Longman, 2004. 333-369. Print.

---. *The Winter's Tale. The Complete Works of Shakespeare* (Fifth Edition). Ed. David Bevington. New York: Pearson Longman, 2004. 1527-1569. Print.

Made in the USA
Middletown, DE
07 February 2015